The Elderly in India

The Elderly in India

Kumudini Dandekar

Sage Publications
New Delhi/Thousand Oaks/London

To the Elderly in India

Copyright © Kumudini Dandekar, 1996

First published in 1996 by

Sage Publications India Pvt Ltd
M-32 Greater Kailash Market I
New Delhi 110 048

Sage Publications Inc
2455 Teller Road
Thousand Oaks, California 91320

Sage Publications Ltd
6 Bonhill Street
London EC2A 4PU

Published by Tejeshwar Singh for Sage Publications India Pvt Ltd, phototypeset by Pagewell Photosetters, Pondicherry, and printed at Chaman Enterprises, Delhi.

Library of Congress Cataloging-in-Publication Data

Dandekar, Kumudini.
    The elderly in India / Kumudini Dandekar.
        p.   cm.
    Includes bibliographical references.
    1. Aged—India. 2. Aged—India—Statistics. I. Title.
    HQ1064.I4D23   305.26′0954—dc20   1996   96–4407

ISBN: 0–8039–9301–3 (US-HB)   81–7036–536–8 (India-HB)

Sage Production Editor: Niti Anand

Contents

List of Tables

Acknowledgements

My thanks are due to Dr. Sharadchandra Gokhale of the Centre for Research and Development, Bombay, for helping me to obtain grants from the Ministry of Social Welfare, Government of India, New Delhi. I am also grateful to Prof. V.M. Dandekar of the Indian School of Political Economy, Pune, for making available to me computer facilities for tabulating the data for the project on which this book is based. I am grateful to the four investigators who carried out the fieldwork, all of whom did their work well; but my especial thanks go to Mrs. Karandikar who has a deep insight into the problems of the old.

Preface

This book attempts to describe the conditions of the old in India, emphasizing the state of Maharashtra. It is assumed that they face a variety of problems including economic, health, non-working status, lack of independence, clash of lifestyles, generation gap and so on. Do these problems differ in rural areas and big cities? Between men and women? Between rich and poor? What is the extent of their health problems and financial stringency? For those many living in stark poverty in their working years, what is their state in their advanced age? Has India as a welfare state any programmes and policies directed to ameliorate the condition of the fast increasing numbers of the elderly?

Today the demographic picture is very strange in India. The average longevity is yet to cross sixty years of age. In 1991 the projected share of the children in the total population was about 35 per cent, and the proportion of elderly about 7 per cent, which is bound to grow rapidly in the coming years. The proportion of the population living in rural areas is still 74 per cent. Though provided with some minimal health facilities, the majority has yet to be given access to the health facilities which are available to urbanites. No form of modernization has yet touched these rural areas. The result is that much of the population lives in a pre-industrialized stage accepting a relatively happy old age, expecting little from the government or any other source. The existence of utter poverty is seen as the continuation of earlier penury. This contrasts with what is happening in the cities, where there is a growth of individualism, and with it the desire to be self-reliant. The clashes between generations that distress the old in the cities are taken in their stride as natural by their rural counterparts. Hence many of the problems facing the urban elderly do not exist for the villagers.

One is not happy with this reaction to old age in rural India though the picture looks relatively problem-free. It seems a core of ignorance needs to dissolve before there is any awakening to the modern view and expectations of old age. As workers involved in the economic and social development of society this seems unsatisfactory to us. One would like to disturb this apathy pervading rural areas. The old do not realize their situation in the absence of knowledge regarding the reasonable expectations of the elderly today. Just as increase in longevity is partly due to economic development, the rising expectations of the old, the growth of individualism, saving for old age or bad days, reducing the burden of too many children to produce fewer better equipped children who not only look after themselves but also help their parents in old age if need be—all these are assumed to be part of economic development. Many of the old we came across were amazed at the idea of saving in their young days for their own old age. This was for two reasons. One was that their earning capacity even in the best of the years was barely adequate for their current needs. Secondly, if there were any savings, these would be utilized for the marriages or education of their children. The elderly in the village never dreamt of saving for their own old age. In fact this idea seemed absurd or crazy to some of them. But such a state of affairs seemed tragic to us in the early nineties.

However a number of other features of village life can be considered healthy. People are not scared of death. They took it as the inevitable. Lacking medication for illness in old age, there is relatively much less medicated survival compared to the situation in the industrially advanced world. The nursing homes of the West sometimes give the impression that they are waiting-rooms for the dead before they are buried. Lying in their beds with a variety of tubes in their bodies, the elderly make a tragic picture of the attempts of modern medication to ward off death. After all, medication has lengthened the lives of people but the reprieved life is not normal. It leaves much to be desired.

Another limitation of medication is that it raises hopes that death can be sidestepped. This has such a pitiable effect on people's attitudes that in certain societies even the terminally ill elderly have to be trained to face inevitable death. In relatively less medicated societies this phenomenon is absent; death is seen as being natural.

The rural world is also small. In it the elderly are inextricably integrated with the life of the village. They are afraid of leaving it.

They believe that it is their village community which will look after them in helpless situations. It will feed them in times of starvation and their trust is not misplaced. We came across a number of situations where helpless elderly lepers or parents of mentally ill elderly children were fed and looked after by the villagers. This attitude and trust are very significant when approaching the problems of the elderly. For instance if an old-age home is to be set up in a rural area, let it have the milieu of community life with which the villagers are familiar.

We also felt that as far as the rural community is concerned, it is better to begin tackling the problem of the helpless old by offering them a monthly pension of say Rs. 100, as is done by the Sanjay Niradhar Anudan Yojana described in the present book. This could help the old to at least buy their food from the neighbouring villagers. This of course is not enough to solve all their problems, but it is a small beginning towards changing the mind-set of the old villagers. The sums needed for this kind of help, i.e., a monthly payment of Rs 100 are not astronomical. In a rural population of about 640 million, about 45 million or 7 per cent are above the age of 60 years. Half of them are poor. Of these about 10 per cent or 2.25 million are helpless, needing old-age pensions. An annual pension of Rs 1,200 per elderly person would amount to Rs 2,700 million for rural India as a whole. The sum does not seem enormous, and such an investment might perhaps change the attitudes of the rural communities towards old age. It is worthwhile pumping in that much money to observe the effects on the rest of society. One question which arises is: Will those living in large families but feeling neglected prefer a comparatively lonely life with a pension? Some may, some may not. But one thing is certain. Rural society will not remain static—with no options for the elderly. One cannot predict whether it will be good or bad. But whatever the consequences, an offer of old-age pensions to the lonely and helpless seems justified. It may introduce a psychological change in both old and young. In old age money is not all. But it is certainly a partial solution. Besides money, medical facilities are required. In addition there are emotional needs. But these are perhaps better satisfied in India than in most parts of the world. With an all-round weakening of abilities, adjustment with the environment is all that is needed, and the Indian rural old are certainly capable of that.

In contrast to the rural population, the city elderly population is quite different. Many from this group have taken recourse to old-age homes. Along with the lonely, the helpless and the destitute, there are those who have differences with their kith and kin, perhaps the next generation, which forced them to leave their own homes and enter the premises of old-age homes. They lead a relatively contented life in these homes, though they often remember their earlier life as a 'golden' past. Their new life in this public environment is no doubt problem-free as far as interrelationships with family members are concerned. But after all it is an institutional life—certainly artificial—being uprooted from one's familiar surroundings and implanted in a strange atmosphere which one has to accept and remain contented with.

Even in India, technological developments have caused tremendous changes in the lifestyles and values of the younger generation in big cities. Their respect for and dependence on the old is reduced. Housing shortage has made the pressures of city life unbearable for the young and even more so for the housebound old, who find their peace of mind threatened. Despite the cramped existence, the old feel lonely and deserted. They feel guilty about being old and housebound. The increase in the employment of women outside the home means their help and presence is lost to the aged in the household.

All the elderly who are weak suffer. But, comparatively, aging brings more miseries to women than men. Poor health, economic dependence, and inability to work lead to a loss of self-esteem. The elderly lose everything including friends, spouses, jobs, status, power, influence, income and health—none of which can be replaced. Thus, they tend to become short-tempered, rigid in their attitudes, selfish and suspicious. Adjustment in the family or society becomes painful. This happens particularly when they come into conflict with the young who are exposed to an urban lifestyle and it leads to isolation. The most affected are the aged widows and widowers.

Many of the problems are due to failing health. Paradoxically, one is afraid that the weeding out process—death of the ill and sometimes terminally ill—resulting from the absence of medication may be weakened with increasing medication in urban areas, so that old-age conflicts may worsen. It seems that two things are needed. One is the offer of old-age pensions to the destitute and the other, the offer of inexpensive housing facilities such as old-age homes for urban dwellers. It is worth noting here that I wrote a few articles on old-age homes in the local newspapers which attracted hundreds of letters from old people in the state of Maharashtra. The feeling persists that our joint family system will last and shelter the old as in a preindustrialized society. But that is more a myth than reality. One cannot follow the Western pattern of economic development with smaller families, emphasis on education, and growth of individualism while maintaining a traditional culture. This will soon be lost because economic development comes in packages.

Going through the material presented in the book, it can be seen that the main problem is poverty, which cannot be easily solved unless old-age security can be offered. Implementing financial assistance is not easy for many reasons. The size of the old-age population is increasing rapidly. Sending old-age pensions to remote areas raises problems such as whether to use the costly money-order system or bank cheques. Banks are not within the easy reach of all.

A positive way of looking at the old is to consider them not as a problem age group but as a fund of experience and skills. This of course is a good approach but not applicable to the majority of the old in India. Even in industrially advanced countries, enormous changes in technology render the old outdated and unemployable. However, there are a number of old people in urban India who are healthy enough to offer their skills to society. In our survey we came across people who were prepared to read to the old and entertain them. They helped the old and the helpless by running errands or doing their marketing for them. Through the efforts of the enlightened old themselves, others can be made aware of contemporary developments. These ideas would of course involve investment as well as sound planning. For instance, the eradication of illiteracy and misconceptions regarding health maintenance can be dealt with by compulsorily sending all retired people from the organized sector to do rural work, the place being left to their choice. Just as medical students have to spend their internship in rural areas before collecting their degree, the retired should collect their retirement benefits only after their rural responsibility of eradication of illiteracy and ignorance has been discharged. Some can organize activities in rural areas or collect data on unemployment or underemployment. Similar work can be carried out in urban slums. While it is obvious that this will not be easy, some such solution will have to be found.

The present study does not cover the poor and underprivileged elderly living in big cities. But one gets some idea about them from those living in old-age homes more or less peacefully.

Pune   Kumudini Dandekar

1

Aging: Hypotheses and Theories

With declining mortality, longevity increases. But the percentage in various age groups tends to remain constant if the birth rate remains the same. The population grows faster due to increasing longevity and a constant percentage means a much larger population in absolute terms. But generally with declining mortality, birth rates start falling after a time lag, leading to enormous changes in the age structure. For instance, people in the industrially advanced countries of the world are approaching a longevity of 80 years. These countries have rates of less than 20 births per 1,000 of population from the rate of about 35 births per 1,000 in the early part of this century. This changed their age ratio structure, with about one-fifth of the population being children, 60 per cent or more working adults, and 15 per cent or more in the older age group. Even in developing countries, once population control becomes evident, the child population percentage could decrease from 40 or thereabouts to 25 or so, and the population of the elderly could increase to 10 per cent or so from the 3 per cent in the early fifties or before. In a country like India child population, which is not yet fully controlled, is still high, constituting more than 35 per cent of the population, and the population of the elderly is increasing to 8 per cent or so. With declining mortality, therefore, India will have to address the question of an increasing population of the old besides that of the young and the attendant problems of crowding, unemployment, undernutrition, and substandard lifestyles. All these issues are so daunting in India that the problem of the old does not stand out as deserving the high priority as is given in industrially advanced countries. But there is also a view that if the problems of old age are squarely faced, with the government providing old-age pension schemes and medical aid, people will be motivated to better control the number of children they have. Once the birth rates come down, most of the above-mentioned problems can be easily solved.

The trend of the size and proportion of population of 60 years of age and above in India is set out in Table 1.1

Table 1.1

Size and Proportion of Population of India in 60+ Age Group in Census Years 1951 to 2001

	1951	*1961*	*1971*	*1981*	*1991*	*2001*
No. of persons (millions)	21	25	33	42	55	76
Percentage of total population	5.7	5.7	6.1	6.5	6.6	7.7

Note: 1991 and 2001 figures are estimated.
Source: Government of India (1988).

As seen from Table 1.1, the number of persons aged 60+ and their percentages are both increasing steadily. This is a cause for concern since the population of the elderly is increasing at a much faster rate than the total population as seen from Table 1.2. In the decade 1981–91 for instance, the percentage increase in the total population was approximately 23.5, while that of the 60+ was 38.02.

Table 1.2

Growth Rates of Total Population and of 60+ Population in India from 1951 to 1991

Period	Per Cent Increase in Total Population	Per Cent Increase in 60+ Population
1951–61	21.51	22.40
1961–71	24.80	32.40
1971–81	24.75	31.60
1981–91	23.50*	38.02

* 1991 census, series 1, provisional population totals.
Source: Same as of Table 1.1.

Considering this rapid increase, it is important to try to project the future size of the aged population and the resulting problems of the old. What is it like to be old? How do people manage the accompaniments of aging, namely, health problems, retirement or widowhood? What is their reaction to death? Various sciences try to find answers to these questions. In the United States of America the interest in aging can be measured by the number of Ph.D. theses in various related subjects. It is significant that research on the old is found in the fields of psychology, education, sociology, economics, language, literature, social work, anthropology, health sciences, nursing, business administration, statistics, geography, political science, public administration, recreation and engineering, with a frequency in that order. The problem of the old seems all-pervading.

The interest in gerontology is enormous. The encyclopaedia of social sciences devotes about 20 pages to aging. The treatment of the old is described among the various cultures of the world from early times, when the old were killed by their relatives, sometimes by the son, perhaps mercifully, so that they could be spared the hardships of a primitive life. It was only when agriculture permitted a settled life that people started taking care of the old.

Three Myths about Old Age

Anthropologist Corinne N. Nydegger (1985: 406) describes three myths showing how an average person looks at the problem of aging. One is the 'golden age of the past' from which modern man has fallen, most often as a consequence of his own sinful acts. The historian Laslett (in Nydegger, 1985: 407, 411) has called this the 'world we have lost' syndrome. The second myth is that of the 'golden island' where things run smoothly as far as the old are concerned. The third is the idea of the 'rosy family'. It is a nuclear family with an intergenerational network that provides strength, love and sustenance in all its members. According to the author these golden ages or rosy families are fabulous constructs. They are wishful thinking. They are unlikely to be true. Actuarial statistics of earlier periods indicate that because of high mortality throughout the life-cycle, few parents attained old age and few children survived to adulthood. Therefore the multigenerational household would have been unusual. Moreover, a number of historians have confirmed that in the English or American past the multigenerational family was rare. Distances posed formidable obstacles unlike the situation today. Mobilization of family members is easy and there seems evidence of much support today for the aged kin.

Moreover, the term 'aged' is not very precise. The aging experience shows gender and class differences. In describing a society, we have to specify which group of the aged we are speaking of—the ill or fit, old in years or only by a generation, male heads of households or widows living on their own, wise leaders or village failures? Generalizations about the esteem in which the aged are held are as superficial or plain wrong in other societies as in our own. One has to keep in mind the following variations in the status of the elderly:

1. All groups of populations have elderly people who are not respected and have little status and power at any age. Not all the elderly get equal treatment. There is competition for position at any age (even between the old and not so old).
2. Only power commands respect.
3. One has to distinguish between societies where only the healthy survive and those where the frail and the weak also survive.
4. Nowhere are the decrepit valued.
5. The elderly sometimes contribute substantially to the household by baby-sitting and kitchen work, but nowhere does it give them social status.
6. Acceptance of and consideration for the elderly varies according to cultural differences, e.g., in Japan in spite of development and modernization, the old are respected. In India in spite of utter poverty, the old are treated well.
7. Only the closest of the kin accept the responsibility of supporting the aged. In fact it is the children. Even in societies where the aged were killed, it was the duty of children to do so. In other words charity begins at home and ends there.

Considering the above, has the myth of the 'golden age of the past' no place? It certainly has. It tells us what ought to be and hence is important. If one wants to generalize the gender distinction, which of course differs from culture to culture, the major difference is that women have the strength to humbly comply with their children's wishes. Otherwise a kind of cold war prevails among the kin relationships.

In simple terms, it must be pointed out that loving, supportive families can be found in all societies. So can their opposites. One has to accept this as natural and attempt to pinpoint those structural features that encourage conflict between members of the family before one can fully understand the aged and their family ties. Presently, there is a movement, mainly in the West, to push back the aged into the bosom of the family. Before that can be done, one should assess realistically the cost to parents and to children of trying to live out a myth.

With the changing role of women—they are increasingly working outside the house—their help to the elderly is going to suffer. It is worthwhile looking at the picture in industrially advanced societies since it could project the future of India. Elaine M. Brody et al. (1985: 424) discuss such changes in women's roles in the US in a study of three generations. These have far-reaching consequences not only for the economy and society but also for the lives of older people and their families. The significance of this will be clear when one notes that 40 per cent of people between 55–59 have at least one living parent, as do 20 per cent of those aged 60–64, and 10 per cent of those aged 65–69. This survey was carried out for the National Teachers' Association by American Association of Retired Persons. One may also note that 90 per cent of the older people with children were grandparents and 46 per cent were great-grandparents. This is significant because traditionally even in the USA, it was the middle-aged women who were the principal providers of care for elderly parents. In India it is the same story. But in big cities women are now going to work outside the household. It is worthwhile studying how far this is likely to affect the care of the old in urban areas as opposed to rural ones. In the USA during 1950–80, the participation of women between the ages 45 and 54 in the labour force rose from 38 per cent to 60 per cent. For those in the 55–64 age group, it rose from 27 per cent to 42 per cent (US Department of Labour in Brody et al., 1985: 424, 434).

As will be seen from the data presented in later chapters, the old, both in India and the industrially advanced countries are not always isolated from their families. Neither are they all in ill health, senile, bored or lonely. One has to give up the idea that they are either gloomy and unfortunate or enjoying 'golden years'. Both are partial truths. It is not that old people start behaving in a given manner at particular age or so. Hence whatever variety one sees in the earlier age groups, one sees in the older ones. Old age is not a straight extrapolation of middle-age. It is affected by health, occupation or activity. In short it depends on the environment in which the old are placed.

Intrinsic and Reactive Effects on the Old

The aging effects resulting from industrialization and its accompaniments are of two kinds: intrinsic and reactive. Intrinsic effects are due to biological changes with aging. Reactive effects arise from social structures including the family structure, which itself is the result of industrialization and other changes. Most old age behaviour is reactive in the sense that it is shaped by social experience. For instance, modernization affects the whole life-cycle, with changes in longevity, health standards, medication, age at marriage, age at retirement, economic circumstances, social security, etc. These affected the attitudes to old age. In rural areas of India, some are surprised to know that governments provided old-age pensions in some regions. They do not expect government intervention even in the worst of circumstances. When told about old-age pensions, they are incredulous.

Sociology of the Aged

An impression has been given that while the aged were treated reverentially in primitive, preindustrial societies, existing in a golden age, they are much worse off in modern societies. They are neglected by their families, forced into boring and meaningless retirement, and derogated by the 'youth culture'. This however is too simplistic a description. The reality of aging in preindustrial societies was often far from idyllic, and many of the stereotypes about the aged living in modern, industrialized societies are exaggerated.

In preindustrialized societies people rarely lived long; e.g., in India only 2 per cent or less lived after 65 in 1951. The definition of 'old' in such societies probably varied. The prestige accorded to the old broadly depended on four components: advisory, contributory, control and residual. The first component comprised the greater experience of the old. The second arose from their participation in cultural, familial and economic activities. The control component arose from their possession of property, practical knowledge and experience. What could be called the residual component depended on their previous status in their communities which also partly included the first component. Thus even in rural India, it was only a few who were respected. One has to note however that in early Indian culture, the smooth transfer of responsibility and control from one generation to the next was sanctioned by the system of ashramas (such as *brahmacharyashram, grihasthashram, wanaprasthashram and sanyasashram*). Parents raised their children, and when the sons married, the responsibility for the family became theirs. However this transition was not always accomplished smoothly because of poverty and urbanization. According to Mahadeo Shastri Joshi (1974), there were two things to be observed in *wanaprasthashram:* (*i*) While handing over the household responsibility without renunciation one should live like a rishi (*ii*) Leaving the son in charge, one should go to a forest to pray to God. However, today there are new problems which are likely to worsen in future. This can be seen even in the well-to-do Indian urban families perhaps due to modernization and the growth of individualism.

Aging in Modern Industrialized Societies

Industrialized societies experience rapid changes, so that the old tend to get outdated fast, while the youngsters perform better in the new, changing set-up. In developed societies too, differences are seen in the conditions of the old depending on various factors such as old-age security measures, health care, and cultural attitudes to the family. Though highly developed, in Japan the old are more highly esteemed than in Western societies. In Japan the old are integrated into the family and community life, while in Western societies, the old living away from the family are not always satisfactorily accommodated. The aged of Japan are likely to continue working; because of the strong work ethic, work after the age of 65 is considered 'normal'. Thus the theory that 'modernization lowers the status of the aged' is proved wrong in the case of Japan. However, the conditions in Japan may change because modernization has been a relatively recent affair there.

Adopting a microapproach to the elderly, their problems may be viewed from the perspective of individual satisfaction. Some scientists have suggested two kinds of theories to view individual cases—the *activity* theory and *disengagement* theory. Activity theory is concerned with the extent to which the old continue their activities of middle age. Disengagement theory can be seen as the opposite of activity theory, concerned as it is with the reasons and consequences of disengagement. The old invariably disengage themselves at various ages, which is good for both the individual and society. Engaging the old is probably more common among the Japanese than in the United States. Generally speaking, in any society no individual was reborn on his 65th birthday, and neither activity nor disengagement could be assumed to be natural way to age. The aging individual makes sense of the present by adapting it in terms of his own past. In India among the majority of rural people engaged in agriculture, people continue working as long as they can (activity theory) and then gradually disengage themselves in preparation for the last phase of life. As aging proceeds, less attention is given to the outside world and a greater preoccupation with inner states is observed.

With the transition of society from the agricultural to the industrial stage, there was an exodus from traditional agricultural practice and the setting of the old changed. In an agrarian set-up, each member of the household has the same source of income. In an industrialized society, on the other hand, an individual wage-earner makes for difficulties in budgeting because of the different sources of income available. Instead of being a productive unit providing for all, the household is now a consumer unit, and those who do not earn are likely to be overlooked when their rights of consumption are assessed. In traditional families the older people accepted the burden of providing for the family, and the next generation living with them could enjoy their incomes if any. But in the non-agricultural context, when the elderly cease to earn they become acutely conscious of their non-earning status and experience a sense of helpless dependency. In urban areas usually it is the old from rural areas that go to live in the son's house. In the urban setting adult children might even take advice from the elderly but might not act on it, knowing that their elderly parents are not sufficiently experienced in the demands of the new setting.

Finally new standards of behaviour, new ways of spending time and money, and the like provide specific grounds for conflict between generations. The disagreements which would have remained suppressed in the past are now openly expressed. Unless the older generation remains silent, suppressing its feelings of disapproval before the young, it risks being subjected to verbal argument and contradiction. Within their cultural framework, this constitutes the antithesis of appropriate modes of intergenerational communication.

In all the above ways, families which include older people are affected by the social transition taking place in urban India. The impact of changes in the economic structure, geographical mobility, education and cultural values is felt at all economic and social levels. But for the poor, especially poor migrants of recent rural origin, these changes threaten the time-tested system of old-age security because aged members of these families have no material power base that can be used to enforce compliance and devotion from their offspring in the face of adverse circumstances.

As we have seen, the rural populace is being pushed out of an agricultural setting into urban areas. All the accompanying ills of this transition are further aggravated by poverty. The traditional family may seem strong. It may also perhaps cushion many of the potentially adverse effects of urbanization on the existing social order. But it is a mistake to think that the future of the family is not changing in an Indian cultural context, given the material conditions in which millions of urbanites lived today. It is not easy to say what solutions can be found. But people must be at least aware about what the future has in store for them. Perhaps this is the first step needed to face the new problems.

Non-Biological Study of the Old

Our examination of the problems of the aged will not enter into a discussion of the biological aspects of human aging. Called primary aging, these factors relate to the biological capabilities of the body. We deal with secondary aging, brought about by external factors like disease, nutrition, stress, etc., which profoundly influence the body's own capabilities. The primary process is immutable, while the secondary process can largely be changed. And it is this change that one would like to assess in different societies. The human body is like a machine run on external energy; it shows signs of wear and tear which are repairable to a certain extent. After some time the machine does not function like new. Similarly the organic cells of the human body fail to function after a span of years. There are a variety of biological hypotheses which cannot be confirmed or refuted since primary and secondary aging cannot be easily separated. The skin, ears, nose and mouth, gastrointestinal tract, cardiovascular system, respiratory system, central nervous system, musculo-skeletal system, endocrine and the immune systems are all affected by aging. The various types of diseases which affect humans in old age are categorized as 'geriatrics'. This is a new branch of medicine which is gaining in importance due to a larger population with greater longevity being exposed to such diseases. However, we will confine ourselves to the socio-demographic profile of the aged.

One may start with the definition of old age. The Department of Social Welfare of the state of Maharashtra brands the aged as *apangas* (i.e., disabled) and clubs them with the physically handicapped. The definition of old age may vary in different contexts, societies and cross-culturally. Old age is often determined by the criterion of retirement from the labour market. In fact labour force participation rates at ages of 60 and above can be compared for various developed and developing countries or for agricultural and non-agricultural communities. However, for a large majority of women who are not considered as being in the labour market or men and women from a big unorganized sector such as agriculture in India, there is no formal age of retirement and hence they cannot be classified in this way.

Norman B. Ryder (1965) suggested that x could be called the age at entry into old age if $e^0_x = 10$. In other words, when only 10 years of average life are left, that age can be called old age. Using this definition, India till 1951 could take the age of 60 as old age. During 1951–81 the age 65 could be taken as old age, and after 1981 the age 70 could be the lower boundary of old age. The Maharashtra Department of Social Welfare, treats 60 years and above as the old age for men, and 55 years for women because many women could be destitute and disabled by that age. But such a flexible definition is very inconvenient for purposes of data analysis. Hence our definition of 'old' in the present work is 60 years and above for both men and women.

It is worthwhile at the outset to scrutinize the demographic setting of the old in India since this will reveal their problems and how they face them. Their ages, marital status, living arrangements, life-cycle, work participation, health standards, and leisure activities will indicate their probable capacity to face old age. The data will also show how they differ from other Indian regions and the industrially advanced world.

We provide in the next chapter the socio-demographic profile of the old in general and in India in particular. The main objective of the present study is to examine the conditions of the old in Maharashtra. Thus, the primary data collected for the present survey covers only this state. While the social milieu of Maharashtra is more or less similar to that of the rest of the country, there are also differences; hence whenever possible the data for the whole country is presented. This enables the information on Maharashtra to be placed in an all-India context.

Chapter 1 is introductory describing the various theories regarding old age. Chapter 2 delineates the socio-demographic profile of the old in India. This includes their age distribution, population growth rates, sex ratio and marital status, health standards, attitudes to children as old-age security, work participation rates, life-cycle in India as compared to that in industrially advanced countries, economic independence or otherwise, leisure activities, and the general level of satisfaction experienced or the problems faced in old age. Chapter 3 is devoted to the data of the National Sample Survey Organization on the old, covering 50,000 households in the country as a whole and 2,200 in the state of Maharashtra. The information is set out for 18 items concerning the old. Presenting the data for all the major states of the country, it is possible in this chapter to examine the interstate variations. Chapter 4 provides data for 19 old-age homes in Maharashtra and carries interviews with a total of 541 inmates of these homes. Chapter 5 concerns the old living in their homes in villages, with 601 interviews of the old villagers. Chapter 6 deals with the Sanjay Gandhi Niradhar Yojana—

the old-age pension scheme in Maharashtra. In Chapter 7 about 30 case-studies of the old are provided. These are intended to reflect the diversity in the old we come across in the present investigation—life-like word pictures which supplement the statistical data presented in earlier chapters.

2

The Socio-Demographic Profile of the Old

This chapter reviews the literature on the socio-demographic conditions of the old. It attempts to place the problems of the old in the larger socio-economic context. Very little literature on the problems of the old in India exists because these problems have not been accorded high priority in this country till recently. The longevity in India had yet to cross the given age of 60 even in the 1981 census. However, one source of data exists, namely, the National Sample Survey (NSS) of 1986–87, 42nd round, which was specially conducted at the instance of the Ministry of Social Welfare, Government of India, to study the conditions of the old. A separate chapter is devoted to this data in this work. Apart from this, only a few examples of data could be found, based on small samples and not always scientifically analyzed. In some states old-age pension schemes have been instituted, but the data pertaining to them are neither published nor easily available. In the industrially advanced countries enormous literature on this subject exists but it is not easily available in our libraries. The present chapter therefore had to be based on scattered data from the Indian censuses, some stray surveys in various regions of the country, and the limited data available on economically developed countries like the United States. A systematic presentation of the problems of the old in India is naturally impossible without adequate data on the subject.

The inclusion of data on the United States is justified because they represent the likely future trend given India's current pattern of industrialization, notwithstanding her high levels of poverty.

In what follows, the census data regarding the old has usually considered the age of 60+ as old age.

How many persons fit the category of 'old' as we have defined it? These are shown for various census years for India and Maharashtra in Table 2.1

Table 2.1
Size and Percentage of Old Population Above 60 Years of Age from 1951 to 2001 in India and Maharashtra

	Census Year					
	1951	1961	1971	1981	1991	2001
No. of persons (millions)						
India	21	25	33	42	55*	76*
Maharashtra	N A	2.08	2.88	4.0	N A	N A
Percentage of total population						
India	5.7	5.7	6.1	6.5	6.6	7.7
Maharashtra	N A	5.2	5.7	6.4	N A	N A

* Estimated.
Source: Government of India (1988).

In 1981 the population of the old in India was 42 million and in Maharashtra 4 million. One may note that the number of old people in India constituted a population more than the combined population of Canada, Australia, and most of the European countries. Even in Maharashtra, the meagre assistance given by the government to the old population, in terms of pension and health maintenance, constitutes a big burden on the economy, if it was helped a little with pension or health maintenance. In other words, whether one looks at the country as a whole or just one state, Maharashtra here, the burden on the exchequer of the old population is heavy, and the economy is not strong enough to bear this load. Moreover as can be seen in Table 2.2, for India the population of the old is increasing at a much faster rate than the total population and is likely to increase much faster in the future.

Faster Increase of Old Population

The same phenomenon of the older population increasing at a faster rate was seen in other countries too. But developing countries

Table 2.2
**Population Growth Rates of Total Population and Old Population
from 1951 to 1991 in India**

Period	Per Cent Increase in Total Population	Per Cent Increase in Population 60 Years of Age & Over
1951–61	21.51	22.40
1961–71	24.80	32.30
1971–81	24.75	31.60
1981–91	23.5	29.00

Source: Same as for Table 2.1.

which showed declining fertility had a faster rate of growth of the older population. Population aging is one of the significant by-products of the so-called demographic transition which has had far-reaching effects, especially in developing countries. It was fertility decline that caused shrinkage of the younger population while the older population increased. In Europe or developed countries this happened very slowly, since decline in fertility was spread over a century or so. Therefore one sees the percentage increases shown in Table 2.3.

Table 2.3
Percentage Increase of the Aged (65 Years and Over) and Other Age Groups for Selected Asian Countries and Areas During 1980–2000

Country	0–14	15–64	65+
World	0.8	2.0	2.3
More developed regions	0.07	0.6	1.3
Less developed regions	0.9	2.4	3.2
Afghanistan	2.4	2.8	2.8
Bangladesh	1.9	3.1	1.6
Burma	1.8	2.7	2.9
China	1.0	2.0	3.1
India	0.4	2.3	3.8
Indonesia	−0.07	2.4	3.1
Japan	−0.01	0.5	3.0
Malaysia	0.8	2.7	3.1
Pakistan	1.8	3.0	2.7
Philippines	1.1	2.8	4.1
Sri Lanka	0.4	2.3	3.6

Source: Rogers (in United Nations, 1985).

Table 2.3 shows that the most dramatic increases in the size of older populations will be in the developing countries. From Table 2.2 it is evident that in India the older population increased faster than the total population. In India as a whole, as well as in Maharashtra, there was a fall in mortality, from above 27 deaths per 1000 population in 1951 to 10 deaths or less in 1991. Births also fell, from 45 or so in 1951 to 30 births or thereabouts in 1991 per 1000 of population. These trends are bound to continue in future, so that the percentage of population less than 15 years of age will decrease to less than 25 or so and the population above 60 years might rise above 10 per cent or so.

Preference of the Old for Rural Living

In 1991 about three-fourths of the old in India live in rural areas (and 61 per cent in rural Maharashtra) about 26 per cent in urban areas (39 per cent in urban Maharashtra). This means that Maharashtra is carrying a relatively bigger load of the urban old and consequently incurring a higher expenditure since the cost of living is higher in urban areas. The rural and urban population of the old in India in 1981 is set out in Table 2.4. The tendency of the old to stay in rural areas is amply clear from the table.

Table 2.4
Distribution of Old Population in India by Location, Age and Sex in 1981

	Rural		Urban		Total	
	Male	*Female*	*Male*	*Female*	*Male*	*Female*
All ages	75.61	77.03	24.39	22.97	100.00	100.00
Age 60+	80.69	80.16	19.31	19.84	100.00	100.00

Source: Registrar-General (1983).

The slightly higher percentage of old females than of males in urban areas could be due to the relatively lower mortality of females in urban areas. But the evidence is not strong. In an industrially advanced country like the United States, the old have a greater tendency to live in urban areas, that too big cities, than in rural areas. However, the old in rural areas constitute a much bigger percentage than persons of all ages. In 1970, for instance,

73 per cent of the old in the United States lived in urban areas and
27 per cent in rural areas, while persons of all ages constituted only
5 per cent or so of those living in rural areas (Ward 1979: 31). In
other words the old everywhere prefer to stay in rural areas more
than those of other age groups.

Sex Ratio of the Old

The sex ratio of the old as opposed to that of total population is of
great interest as it indicates the differential mortality in the two
sexes. In all populations the sex ratio (females to males), especially in
old age is much more favourable to females than to males. In
most of the advanced countries females live longer than men by
four to even eight years or so. This phenomenon affects the sex
ratio. Thus, in the United States men were fewer than 70 per cent
of women at age of 65 and over; less than 60 per cent or so of
women at age 75 and over; and less than 50 per cent or so for ages
85 and over in 1980 (Ward, 1979: 30).

In Table 2.5 the percentage of males and females in various
countries in 1980 shows how India stands out markedly in having a
much smaller percentage of old women as compared to men. It
obviously throws enormous light on their higher mortality, compared
to that of men, and their low status in society. In fact, these
percentages indicate that elderly Indian women are the least
advantaged compared to those in other countries. However, in old
age females were larger in number than females in all ages as seen
in Table 2.6.

Table 2.5
Percentage of the Aged Males and Females in Different Countries in 1980

Country	Aged 60–69		Aged 70–79		Aged 80+	
	Male	Female	Male	Female	Male	Female
Australia	44.8	55.2	38.4	61.6	32.7	67.3
Egypt	46.3	53.7	44.3	55.7	41.7	58.3
France	40.7	59.3	32.8	67.2	28.6	71.4
India	51.7	48.3	51.1	48.9	49.9	50.1
Japan	43.0	57.0	41.9	58.1	37.2	62.8
Nigeria	45.2	54.8	43.7	56.3	40.6	59.4

Table 2.5 (Continued)

Country	Aged 60–69		Aged 70–79		Aged 80+	
	Male	*Female*	*Male*	*Female*	*Male*	*Female*
Sweden	44.9	55.1	40.8	49.2	37.3	62.7
United Kingdom	41.8	58.2	33.9	66.1	28.3	71.7
USA	42.8	57.2	36.7	63.3	33.4	66.6
World	43.9	56.1	41.6	58.4	37.1	62.9

Source: Provisional Projections of the United Nations Population Division, New York (1979–80).

Table 2.6
Sex-ratio in India, Females per 1000 Males in Censuses by Age

Ages	Census Years			
	1951	*1961*	*1971*	*1981*
All ages	946	941	930	933
60–69	993	967	921*	981
70+ years	1,042	1,064	970	974

* Figure not certain.
Source: Government of India (1988).

In short, older populations all over the world are predominantly female, though it will take some years before this becomes true for India. The low status of Indian women is well-known though its effect on mortality is expected to decline in future. However, the biological basis of better longevity for females is seen even in India as indicated by the available data. For instance, the expected longevity after 60, 65 and 70, derived from the life tables for Indians and denoted by e^0_{60}, e^0_{65} and e^0_{70} in Table 2.7 for males and females in various census years, is higher for women than men.

This phenomenon is observable not only in the life table population but also in the age distribution at various years as seen in Table 2.8.

Thus among the old, females are predominant not only in other parts of the world, but also in India in spite of the relatively higher mortality among them compared to the rest of the world. The percentage of widows among old women is much higher than the

Table 2.7
The Expected Longevities for Men and Women in Various Census Years After 60, 65, and 70 Years of Age

Census year	e^0_{60}		e^0_{65}		e^0_{70}	
	Male	Female	Male	Female	Male	Female
1901–11	9.0	9.3	7.3	7.6	5.8	6.0
1911–21	9.0	9.5	7.3	7.7	5.8	6.2
1921–31	9.3	9.9	7.5	8.0	6.0	6.4
1931–41	10.0	10.6	8.0	8.6	6.3	6.8
1941–51	10.9	11.4	8.8	9.2	6.8	7.3
1951–61	12.3	12.8	9.8	10.3	7.6	8.0
1961–71	14.0	14.3	11.1	11.5	8.6	8.9
1971–81	16.1	16.1	12.8	13.0	9.7	9.9
1981–91	17.3	18.0	13.7	14.5	10.4	11.0
1991–2001	18.3	20.0	14.6	15.9	11.0	12.1

Source: Malaker and Roy and, Demographic Research Unit, Indian Statistical Institute (1986).

Table 2.8
Percentage of Population at Ages 60+, 65+ and 70+ in India for the Years 1950–2000

	Males			Females		
	60+	65+	70+	60+	65+	70+
1950	5.2	2.9	1.7	6.1	3.8	2.0
1960	5.5	3.3	1.7	5.8	3.5	1.9
1970	5.9	3.6	1.9	6.0	3.7	2.0
1980	6.4	4.0	2.2	6.6	4.1	2.3
1990	7.1	4.5	2.5	7.6	4.8	2.8
2000	8.0	3.5	3.0	8.9	5.9	3.4

Source: United Nations (1988).

percentage of widowers because of the higher longevity of women at older ages and husbands being generally older than wives.

Moreover compared to women, widowed men are more likely to remarry; hence the percentage of widowed women is much higher than that of widowers among the old, in India as well as elsewhere. Table 2.9 for 1981 census reveals how the marital status of men and women in India differs.

Table 2.9
**Percentage in 1981 of Married, Widowed and Divorced or Separated
at Older Ages by Sex**

Age Group		Currently Married	Widowed	Divorced or Separated
60–64	M	83.44	14.13	0.39
	F	43.17	55.98	0.48
65–69	M	80.58	17.06	0.38
	F	40.79	58.41	0.41
70+	M	70.45	27.12	0.39
	F	21.72	77.57	0.30

Note: A very large percentage of widowed women among the old reflects their status in the family.

Living Arrangements of the Old

Where do the old live? Do they live with their children? Or do they live independently? What follows is largely a review of literature on the subject in the industrially advanced countries, for which data is available. For India, and separately for Maharashtra, not much data is available. Stray surveys reveal that in a country like India, old men and women are likely to live with their children to a much larger extent than in industrialized countries. Similarly, living only with the spouse is also not as common in India as elsewhere in the advanced world. But there is a feeling that in Indian cities the conditions are changing. Even if unwanted, the old have to live with their children since most of them cannot afford to have independent households. While the available data on the subject for India is inadequate, it has been provided to illustrate the differences between the Indian conditions and those elsewhere. Thus in a city like Madras, the living arrangements of the old can be seen from Table 2.10 in a 1972 survey.

A very small percentage lived alone in Madras city. About half of the men or women lived with married sons and daughters as seen in Table 2.10. Similar data for an Italian city (Milan) for 1960 for the 65+ aged persons in Table 2.11 brought out the difference between Madras and Milan. In Madras a relatively much larger percentage lived with their children and even married sons compared to women in Milan as far back as thirty years ago. Similarly

Table 2.10
Living Arrangements of Aged Persons (60+) by Sex (Percentages)

	Men	*Women*	*Total*
Alone	2	3	3
Only with spouse	8	1	5
With married son	39	39	39
With married son and daughter	4	5	4
With married daughter	10	23	17
With unmarried child	25	7	15
With siblings	5	6	5
With grandchildren	1	4	3
With other relatives	5	10	8
With non-relatives	1	2	1
Total	100	100	100

Source: School of Social Work (in Bose, 1982).

Table 2.11
Living Arrangements of Old (65+) in Milan City (Italy) by Sex

	Men	*Women*
Alone	7.6	20.3
With spouse	45.4	18.6
With spouse and one or two children	20.1	8.0
With son	3.0	11.0
With daughter	6.1	13.4
With children	1.7	3.0
With married children	6.1	9.9
With relatives	4.8	9.3
With others	2.6	2.8
No reply	0.2	0.1
Total	97.6	96.4

Source: Ernest W Burgess (in Bose, 1982).

the percentage of women living alone in Milan was comparatively much higher than in Madras since they could afford it. Living only with spouse was also more common in Milan than in Madras. But this need not lead us to the conclusion that the old in the industrialized world do not need their children's proximity. The data in Table 2.12 is very significant from this point of view. One can see

Table 2.12
**Proximity of the Nearest Child to People Aged 65 and Over in
Great Britain, USA and Denmark**

Proximity of Nearest Child	*People with Living Children (percentages)*		
	Britain	*USA*	*Denmark*
Same household	41.9	27.6	20.1
10 minutes journey or less	23.5	33.1	32.0
11–30 minutes journey	15.9	15.7	23.0
31–60 minutes journey	7.6	7.2	12.4
Over 1 hour but less than a day	9.1	11.2	11.2
One day journey or more	1.9	5.2	1.3
Total number	1,911	2,012	2,009

Source: Stehonwer (1965: 147).

that even in the advanced world, including Britain, USA and
Denmark, more than 50 per cent of old people lived either in the
same household as a child or 10 minutes or less distance from the
child. Thus the difference between a country like India and the
advanced countries is that the latter could afford to establish
separate households to a much larger extent. Moreover, while due
to the growth of individualism they lived separately, they still
probably needed their children's proximity. This human element
remained in spite of better levels of living.

Therefore it is difficult to substantiate the idea that in industrialized countries relations between children and parents do not exist.
The parents certainly appreciate the vicinity of children, even
though they live separately in substantial numbers. Another myth
that 'in advanced countries the old live in old-age homes' also
needs to be dispelled because the percentage living in institutions
was not large as seen in Table 2.13. One has to remember that the
rates in the table are per 1000. Thus in the age group 65–74 years,
only 1 per cent or so were institutionalized. The percentage was
about 5 in the age group 75–84, and 20 in the age group 85+.
Moreover, more females than males were institutionalized. They
were perhaps widows. It is significant that even in the USA the
percentage institutionalized was substantial only in the 85+ age
group, when the old involved were likely to be terminally ill with
nobody to look after them. Otherwise old people too had their
own homes (though sometimes poor) as shown in Table 2.14.

Table 2.13
Rate of Institutionalization per 1000 in Nursing and Personal Care Homes by Age and Sex

Age group	Total	Male	Female
All ages (20+)	6.5	4.2	8.5
20–64	0.9	0.9	0.9
65–74	11.6	9.9	12.9
75–84	51.7	36.9	62.3
85+	203.2	130.8	247.6

Source: US Public Health Service (in Ward, 1979: 388).

Table 2.14
Living Arrangements of Persons 65 and Over by Sex in 1975 (Percentages)

	Male	Female
In families	79.8	56.1
Head of the family	76.1	8.5
Other relatives	3.7	12.7
Wife	–	35.0
Living alone	14.8	37.3
Living with unrelated individuals	1.2	1.2
In an institution	4.2	5.3

Source: US Bureau of Census (in Ward, 1979: 50).

According to Russell A. Ward the old lived even in dilapidated houses in order to cling to their own homes in preference to living in old-age homes.

As seen in Table 2.14, only 5 per cent or so of men and women lived in institutions. It was this institutionalization which fell into disrepute and led to the spread of horrific stories about the handling of the old in the United States. Consequently, a lot of literature came out in the USA on the kinds of institutions that were available and what was the effect on the old of residing in them. These institutions were mostly nursing homes whose number tripled during 1960–70; by 1974 there were 23,000 nursing homes in the United States housing over 1 million old people (Ward, 1979: 391). The number of such nursing homes increased because of the profits they could make assisted by the medicare and medicaid enactment of 1965. In 1974, 60 per cent of the income of the nursing home industry came from medicare and medicaid. Seventy-five per cent of the nursing homes were profit-making, while the rest were run by voluntary organizations such as churches. Thus the serious question of the old was left to the free market. Governmental commission arrangements with pharmacists or laboratories, which increased profits from the nursing homes, were common. Poor hygiene, malnutrition, inadequate records and lack of preventive and emergency care plagued these nursing homes. They were short of professional staff including nurses. Inmates of such nursing homes, if relocated, died at a higher rate. It was debatable whether the nursing homes solved more problems than they caused, and therefore some countries offered home-help services (both personal and health care) rather than old-age nursing homes. In India old-age homes are few. They house 0.68 per cent of the old as recorded in the data from the National Sample Survey Organization 42nd round, July 1986–June 1987. Chapter 4 is devoted to the kind of old-age homes found in Maharashtra.

The kind of services required by and available to the old in the United States is worth noting. The federal government provided the following kinds of services to the old: (*i*) ensuring adequacy of income through social security; (*ii*) provision of non-cash benefits such as medicare; (*iii*) protection of the rights of the aged; (*iv*) financing of research and training; (*v*) financial support to public and private organizations at the state and local level; (*vi*) coordination of the above. Per capita expenditure for health in 1975 for those above 65 years showed a ratio of 34 per cent private to 66 per cent public (Ward, 1979: 425). The United States being a rich country, substantial help was forthcoming from the public to the old. The conditions in India and specifically Maharashtra will be described later in this book.

Living with Sons

In India the problem of old-age security was solved by living with sons or relatives. In Korea out of 1,856 persons aged 60 and above, 79 per cent were living with their children. Such percentages of course seem to decline with modernization. For instance in South Korea, according to a Gallup poll of 1984, 83 per cent had expressed a desire to live together as a whole family. But the percentage declined to 61.4 by 1990 (Ehn Hyum Choe, 1992). In Malaysia 72 per cent, and in Philippines 79 per cent, were living with their children according to a WHO study (Andrews et al., 1986). Naturally the attitude of the parents in many Asian countries in the past was to ensure their old-age security by having as many sons as possible. That is why in all the studies in India conducted during 1950–70 regarding attitudes to childbearing, one could see pro-natalist tendencies; old-age security through sons was the important determinant of the decision regarding family size. Such studies were called KAP studies (i.e., Knowledge of family planning methods, Attitude to family planning, and Practice of family planning). A more recent study, conducted among 300 relatively poor, Scheduled Caste persons and 300 relatively well-to-do, non-Scheduled Caste persons of age 60+ (Pati and Jena, 1989: 133–42) brought out this dependence on children with increasing poverty. Thirty-eight per cent of the Scheduled Caste old live with married sons, while among the non-Scheduled Castes, the percentage is only 26. When asked how many children they wanted, the Scheduled Castes mentioned three sons and two daughters, while non-Scheduled Castes two sons and one daughter on an average. Among the Scheduled Castes, 96 per cent were prepared to continue having children till a son was born while non-Scheduled Castes were prepared to do so in 53 per cent of the cases.

A study of 100 pensioners in Tirupati (in Andhra Pradesh state of India) was conducted around 1987–88. These were state, central government, or quasi-government pensioners. They were asked how far they expected their children to help them and how much help they received. It was found that less than half the people were satisfied with the support they received from their sons. Support from two working sons was not necessarily greater compared to that from one working son. With the advance of old age, daughters were found to help better in times of crisis. The study suggested that increasing the number of children does not ensure more support during old age. On the other hand, better support was forthcoming from a smaller number provided the children were better equipped to provide it. This strengthens the argument that a small family norm should be accepted.

Children, particularly sons, as a source of security in old age is worth examining, especially among those with limited longevity, poorly educated children, and a low earning capacity. This question can be better studied by examining the life-cycles of families and observing the differences between the developed and developing countries.

Family Life-Cycle

The decline in birth and death rates affected not only the age structure of the populace, but also the family make-up and the so-called family cycle. The idea behind the concept of family cycle is that families are affected by the series of events comprising births of children, their education and other responsibilities, their entry into the labour force, their marriages, and how long all these responsibilities continue. Is there time left to enjoy the care and support from one's offspring? How much time will one have to earn for one's old age? Studies of such life-cycles are not available for India. One carried out by Kingsley Davis and Pietronella Van Den Oever (in Pati and Jena, 1989: 255) brings out the intercountry differences in life-cycles, as seen in Table 2.15 below.

Table 2.15
Comparison of Aging in India in 1956 and the United States in 1880 and 1950

	North India 1956	*US 1880 Cohort*	*US 1950 Cohort*	*Rural India* 1990*
Years from the Birth of the first child to age 18 of the last child	36.8	27.9	24.9	29
Years from age 18 of the last child to death of the mother	None	21.3	34.1	10

* Estimated by the present author.

The responsibilities of Indians even in 1956 extended for a longer period (36.8 years) than of those in the US in 1880 (27.9 years). Near about the middle of the twentieth century the period of responsibilities for children in the United States was two-thirds of that in India in 1956. But Indian mothers died before their responsibility regarding their children's education or their employability was completed, while Americans had ample time to plan their old age. Research shows that in 1956 before the children became skilled and employable, Indian mothers were forced to leave them in order to somehow eke out a living. This meant that the old in India worked till they died unless forced to retire for health reasons. The corresponding picture of India in 1990 may be constructed as follows: if one assumes the first child to be born when the mother was 19 and the last at 30, the Indian mother was living for 10 years on an average after the last child was 18, if the longevity of the mother is assumed to be 58. This means ten years of carefree life for the mother. Had the children been properly educated and made employable, the 1990 picture would have shown Indian mothers being able to plan their own old-age security with the help of 10 years of responsibility-free work. But in India of 1990 the employability of the children was only at the minimum subsistence level, so that they could not take care of their parents; nor were the mothers old enough to be grouped as old.

There are two more similar life cycles. Of these, one was elaborately described by Shigemi Kono (1977). These two cycles are set out in Table 2.16.

Table 2.16
Median Ages of Japanese Women at Selected Stages of the Family Life-cycle in Japan and the Assumed Cycle in India, 1990

Stage	1940 Japan	1972 Japan	1990 India*
Birth	0.0	0.0	0.0
Graduation from school	14.5	18.5	Just literacy
First marriage	20.8	23.1	18
Birth of first child	23.2	25.3	19
Birth of last child	35.5	27.9	30
Start of schooling of last child	42.0	34.4	36
Last child's entrance into university	56.0	46.4	No entry except in unskilled work
Graduation of last child	59.0	50.4	No graduation
Marriage of last child	58.3	52.5	50
Death of husband	42.9	67.1	55+
Death of herself	49.6	75.5	58

* Estimated by the present author.
Source: Kono (1977).

In 1940 a Japanese woman could survive for only 14 years after the birth of the last child. In 1972 she could survive for 48 years in the corresponding situation. In 1940, the death of the husband, 7 years after the birth of the last child was the normal expectation in Japan. In 1972 a husband could expect to live for another 40 years. In 1940 the husband was expected to die less than a year after the last child started grade school, and when the last child got married both parents would be dead. In contrast in 1972 there was no possibility of the husband dying before the marriage or graduation of the last child. Thus the change in Japan was no doubt dramatic and many of the highly developed countries resemble the Japan of 1972.

A similar picture of the life-cycle in India in 1990 can be drawn. If the age at marriage is assumed to be 18, the birth of the first child can be estimated at 19. The last child would be born when the mother is 30 and the child would marry when she is near about 50. Widowhood can be expected at 55 or so and her own death at about 58. The differences between this cycle for India and the two cycles for Japan are worth noting. As far as longevity is concerned, the mothers or parents are doing just right in India, in the sense that both the parents see their children through. But the main problem was *how* do they see their children through? On an average child girls are still illiterate and boys are educated to just above literacy level. This level of education and equipment does not lead to their early self-reliance. What at best they achieve is 'eking out a living somehow' which they do almost till the end of their lives. They hardly save anything for their old age and thus will hardly be capable of taking care of their old parents. In short, the 1990 picture of India does not look so bleak because of the relatively shorter longevity of 60 years or less. But in future longevity is bound to increase, and if by that time people have not learnt to save for their old age, they will be doomed since there will neither be any old-age security nor any help from one's own savings. Therefore, what is badly needed is to start saving for old age before greater longevity of beyond 60 years or so occurs. The capacity to save can come from two sources. First, by reducing the load of child dependency, and second, by equipping everyone with adequate education and employment skills. With the prevailing poverty conditions, these sources are not available—low incomes mean that more hands are needed to keep the home fires burning, but a larger number of children makes the task of educating them that much more difficult. Hence the small family is a must if in future longevity is going to increase. Otherwise with the present poor educational skills, if greater longevity occurs, greater suffering will ensure. Ideally, having two children before the age of 28 will enable the people to live with some decency in old age. If the past life-cycle pattern continues, old people will have to live a longer part of their lives with malnutrition and bad health since whatever happens longevity is going to increase in the future.

Work Participation of the Old

Given India's present longevity, near about 60 or less, many of the problems of old age have been avoided. Those who had good health continued to live and work, while those with bad health were rapidly weeded out since medication was mostly unavailable. People worked till death in the majority of cases out of need. The work participation rates in India in the censuses of 1971 and 1981 are shown in Table 2.17.

Table 2.17

Work Participation Rates of Main Workers for All Ages and for Age 60 and Above in 1971 and 1981

Age group		Male		Female	
		1971	1981	1971	1981
All ages	T	52.61	51.62	12.06	13.99
	R	53.62	52.62	13.36	16.00
	U	48.80	48.54	6.62	7.28
60 and above	T	73.82	63.88	10.64	10.15
	R	77.52	67.78	11.49	11.27
	U	55.35	47.60	6.46	5.63

Source: Government of India (1988).

In 1971 among those aged 60 and above, more than three-fourths of the rural population worked; this proportion fell to two-thirds in 1981. In urban areas more than half (55 per cent) worked after 60 years of age in 1971 and 48 per cent were working in 1981. The percentage working after the age of 60 reduced appreciably during 1971–81. Thus people retired from work more often in 1981 than in 1971. In 1986–87, in the 42nd round of the National Sample Survey, the trend during 1971–81 was maintained, reducing the percentage working both in rural and urban areas. Work and retirement were the subjects most studied in the industrially advanced countries. But not so in India. There were however understandable reasons for this. In India the unorganized sector still occupied a major percentage of the population (more than three-fourths); therefore there was no forced or unnatural retirement. Depending on their health, people retired naturally when they began their non-productive roles. Thus in India there was no period between retirement and disablement by aging which created distress in the modern period even in the urban sector. This period gave meaning to the aging process. Certain types of people were more likely to continue working: those with a high level of education, high occupational status, and those who were still married. In certain matters, older workers worked better than the younger ones.

The employment pattern of the aged, i.e., those above 60 years of age, in other Asian countries was similar. For instance in Bangladesh and Indonesia, more than 60 per cent of males aged 65 and above were in the workforce (Linda Martin in Pati and Jena, 1989: 32, 36). Thus men were largely economically independent if they earned enough, and women were mainly dependent on children or others. In India the economic condition of the old became a major issue, which made all other issues fade into insignificance.

The male and female labour force participation rates in developed and developing countries generally are set out in Table 2.18. They reveal that work participation in old age in developing countries is much higher than in the developed countries.

Table 2.18
Work Participation Rates in Developed and Developing Countries

Area and Age Group	Percentage Active					
	1950		1975		2000	
	M	F	M	F	M	F
Developed countries						
45–54	95	44	94	60	93	67
55–64	86	32	75	32	69	35
65+	44	17	23	8	17	6
Developing countries						
45–54	97	39	95	46	93	44
55–64	91	31	84	35	77	30
65+	69	16	53	17	34	10

Source: ILO (1979).

It seems that with economic development, males start working less, especially in old age. The same is not necessarily so among females. For instance the male/female participation rates in the United States are shown in Table 2.19.

Table 2.19
Labour Force Participation (Excluding Institutionalized Population)
by Age and Sex during 1900–75 (United States)

	1900	1950	1960	1975
Males				
55–64	93.3	86.9	86.8	75.8
65+	68.3	45.8	33.1	21.7
Females				
55–64	14.1	27.0	37.2	41.0
65+	9.1	9.7	10.2	8.3

Source: US Bureau of the Census (in Ward, 1979: 53).

The proportion of older men working has declined from two-thirds in 1900 to less than one-fourth in 1975. Retirement in the United States at least is a twentieth century phenomenon. The reasons for this trend are voluntary and compulsory retirement programmes, pension systems, social security, and changes in the occupational structures, besides of course the rising mean age of the old. However one must remember that 22 per cent of males still worked, which meant retirement was not inevitable. Still, the distinction between agricultural and industrial societies set off the difference in the way these two kinds of societies aged. Retirement in developed societies was viewed as a crisis having profound social and psychological consequences in the lives of older persons, some of whom dreaded retirement.

More Intensive Poverty in Old Age

Retirement led to poverty in many cases, especially in a country like India where even in full adulthood many people were only eking out a living. Those who had saved a little in younger days as a provision for the future also experienced poverty in old age due to continuing inflation, expenditure on medicines, marriages and deaths. Even in a rich country like the United States, the problem of poverty in old age prevailed. Fostering the negative attitudes of the old, financial problems often existed. For instance semi-skilled and unskilled people were unwilling to retire due to poverty. Low income was the greatest problem of old age. In a survey conducted by the National Council on the Aging (Washington DC), old people were asked to note the things they missed most in retirement, their replies are indicated in Table 2.20.

Table 2.20
Things Missed by Retired People of 65 and Over About Their Jobs

	Missed	Did Not Miss	Not Sure	One Thing Missed Most
Money that is Brought	74	24	2	28
The people at work	73	25	2	28
The work itself	62	36	2	10
Feeling of being useful	59	38	2	11
Things happening around you	57	39	4	5
Respect of others	50	45	5	2
Having a fixed schedule every day	43	54	3	4

Source: Louis Harris and associates (in Ward, 1979: 197).

Table 2.20 shows that it is no wonder that 'money' is the one thing missed most by old people. Even in the United States, one in five of the old had a retirement income below the poverty level and as many as three-fourths lacked an adequate income. Financial security was a major determinant of satisfaction in old age. In India today people depend on sons or children in old age as they did in the United States in 1800 when a couple needed four children to be 95 per cent certain that a male child would survive until the parents' old age (Ward, 1979: 208). A national survey in the mid-seventies found that only 11 per cent of adults between 18–64 felt that children should support their parents during retirement. That is why the family size had declined in the USA (National Council on Aging; in Ward, 1979: 369).

Poverty or inadequacy of income leads to dependence on children in old age. For those with land to cultivate, the son can be relied upon; others have to depend on their own labour or that of their

children. It is not enough to provide for one's own children as well
as the old parents. Moreover, poverty in India is so severe that
people tend to live from day to day. Incomes are inadequate to
meet the two responsibilities of raising children and taking care of
aging parents. Further even if old-age pension was to be offered,
after 65 years of age people will continue to depend on children.
People should be made to realize that a measure such as education
taken 'now' will help them 'now' by reducing the burden of child
dependency. That is why 'adult education' should strongly
emphasize the importance of education in childhood; otherwise
unemployed or underemployed persons will produce only unemployable progeny and poverty will continue. If old-age security
were to be assured to the old, it might tend to change the attitudes
of the young to their own children. One has to remember that
gradually the dependency load which is now heavy on account of
childhood dependency was going to be heavy from the old age
group. For instance, J.P. Ambannavar (in Pati and Jena, 1989:
110) has estimated the dependency ratios for 1971–2021, with
medium population projection, by using ratios P 0–14/P 15–59 and
P 60+/P 15–59 (P for population). The former dependency ratio is
of age group 0–14 to working age population and the latter of old
people to working age population. The ratios are presented in
Table 2.21 for India.

Table 2.21
Dependency Ratios in 1971–2021 for India

Year	0–14/15–59	60+/15–59	Total Dependency
1971	78.0	9.6	87.6
1981	71.9	9.9	81.8
1991	64.4	10.8	75.2
2001	55.7	11.9	67.6
2011	46.6	13.0	59.6
2021	40.0	15.7	55.7
2081	34.7	36.1	70.8

One may note that with the gradual fall in the birth rates, the
dependency load of rearing children decreased, that of providing
for the old increased, and still total dependency decreased. The
same total when estimated for 2081 increased to 70.8 as shown in
the last column.

The poverty of the old is well-known and is found even among the rich countries such as the United States as mentioned above. One sees it in India too and it is not surprising. A survey of 600 persons half from Scheduled Castes and half from non-Scheduled Castes, in Pati and Jena (1989: 133–42) above 60 years of age was conducted in South Central India. The Scheduled Castes were more dependent on wage labour and the data, presented in Tables 2.22 to 2.25, show that they were poorer and their poverty led to the relative lack of respect from their children as seen in their share in decision-making. A survey conducted among agricultural landholders and labourers revealed similar conditions, labourers being the poorer (Pati and Jena, 1989: 151–65).

Table 2.22
**Resource Adequacy of the Old Among Scheduled Castes (SC)
and Non-Scheduled Castes (NSC)**

Resource Adequacy	NSCS	SCS
High enough	29.33	15.00
Just enough	50.00	35.00
Not enough	20.67	50.00

Source: Pati and Jena (1989: 140).

Table 2.23
**Basic Necessities Satisfied or not, Among the Old of Scheduled
Castes (SC) and Non-Scheduled Castes (NSC)**

Response	Food		Clothing		Medical Attention		Recreation	
	NSC	SC	NSC	SC	NSC	SC	NSC	SC
Fully satisfied	48	15.6	46	18	15	10	16	25
Partially satisfied	50	80.4	54	78	75	65	59	55
Not satisfied	2	4.0	–	4	10	25	25	20.9

Source: Pati and Jena (1989: 138).

In old age health is bound to fail, sooner or later. The 36th round of the National Sample Survey in 1983 provided a great deal of data on the health of old people. While these have not been dealt with in this work, the health data of the 42nd round are analysed in the next chapter.

Table 2.24
Remittances from Employed Children to the Old Among Scheduled Castes and Non-Scheduled Castes

Remittances	NSCS	SCS
Remit	54.52	46.39
Do not remit	45.48	53.61

Source: Pati and Jena (1989: 139).

Table 2.25
Decisions in the Families of Scheduled Castes and Non-Scheduled Castes

Decision	NSCS	SCS	Total
Totally decided by the aged	48.33	15.67	32.05
Decided in consultation with the aged	35.90	39.00	37.45
Decided without consulting the aged	15.77	45.33	30.50
Total	100.00	100.00	100.00

Source: Pati and Jena (1989: 136).

Given India's nutrition and poverty levels, the health of her citizens is bound to be poor. Inadequate medical attention during illness means low survival rates, leading to relatively shorter longevity. Medicated survival at older ages is relatively absent in India except among a handful of rich people. However, it could be that the onset of old age is much earlier in India. This aspect is dealt with in the chapter on NSS data on health.

Mental illness is another aspect of old age which might need attention. The incidence of mental illness among old people is reported to be much higher than among the young. In the New Castle Study (Kay et al. in Pati and Jena, 1989: 144), it was established that one in ten over the age of 65 had an organic brain syndrome. Half of them were suffering from senile dementia and the other half from arteriosclerotic dementia. Functional disorders in the aged are more widespread. One in three people over 65 was affected with this. Half of this population suffered from neurotic disorders requiring supportive mental health care. Mental disorders in old age are quite common. The causes are complex, multiple and complicated by organic brain involvement. Failure in social and personal adaptation, cultural breakdown, and losses and

bereavements lead to the disintegration of personal lives. Acceptance of old age within the community, attitudes of children and
grandchildren, and religious beliefs and acceptance of death as
well as disease all play their role in the changing frames. Treatment
from family members and key relations affect the course and
treatment of the mentally ill. There are no data on these problems
for India.

Old-Age Security

Old-age security is another aspect of old age which needs to be
addressed. In India and many other developing countries old-age
security is not available for the unorganized sector which includes
mainly the agricultural workforce. Recently the conditions have
been changing. In India too, many of the states are offering old-
age pensions to those employed in the agricultural sector. In
Maharashtra in October 1980 an old-age pension scheme, called
Sanjay Niradhar Anudan Yojana, was started for men above 65
years and women above 60. This will be dealt with thoroughly in
Chapter 6 of this book.

Social security schemes were instituted much earlier in Western
European countries. Schemes began in 1889 in Germany, 1906 in
Austria, 1908 in Great Britain, and 1913 in Sweden (Ward, 1979:
208). By 1973 at least 105 countries had some type of old age/
invalidity/survivors programme. The United States was a late-
comer in the provision of such insurance. This was because there
was a fear that it would lead to socialism. During the depression of
thirties however there was a growing recognition of poverty among
the aged and social security programmes got more support. With
the Social Security Act of 1935, the United States became the last
major industrial country to establish a public retirement pension.
This measure was taken to give old people a pension, retire them,
and make room for younger workers. In 1948 only 13 per cent of
all people aged 65 and over were receiving social security payments.
This has risen to about 80 per cent of all old people in the early
nineties.

In the national poll conducted for the National Council on
Aging (in Ward, 1979: 369) 81 per cent in the US held that old
people should be supported by the government, 76 per cent that

they should be provided enough to live comfortably, and 97 per cent agreed that there should be cost-of-living increases for social security. Social security was the major source of income for nearly 60 per cent of those over 65. In 1966, 60 per cent of all recipients would have been below the poverty line without this assistance, and 90 per cent of these were raised from poverty by their income from social security (Ward, 1979: 209).

The reasons given for retirement (Table 2.26) by the social security beneficiaries in the United States between 1951 and 1963 are worth examining to get an idea of the changes that were occurring during this period. It is significant that poor health was a major reason for retirement in the United States. As for India the relevant data are presented in great detail in the following chapter based mainly on National Sample Survey data.

Table 2.26
**Reasons for Retirement in 1951 and 1963 Given by Social Security
Beneficiaries in the United States**

Reason for Retirement	1951	1963
I. Own decision	54	61
Poor health	41	35
Preferred leisure issue	3	17
Other reasons	10	9
II. Employer's decision	46	39
Compulsory retirement	11	21
Poor health	7	6
Laid off or job discontinued	22	8
Other reasons	6	4

Source: Erdman Palmore (in Ward, 1979: 186).

In concluding this chapter one is very aware of the paucity of literature on the subject of the old. However, while the data on the old are 'spotty', they are sufficient to identify the problems of the old. The censuses reveal the phenomenon of a faster increasing old population, and one needs to be aware of the need to face the problems of the old soon. The preference of the old for rural living is also seen in the census data. There is a great need for improving the living conditions in rural localities, especially the medical services.

The strong predominance of older women compared to older men is universal. But in India this phenomenon is reversed, probably due to the higher mortality among women than men. It speaks volumes about women's low status in India and the measures needed to improve it. Living arrangements emphasize the well-known fact of the Indian old living with their children—sons in particular. Sons are the strongest support in old age, promoting the pro-natalist attitude of Indians. Therefore some kind of old-age pension schemes have to be offered to people even in the unorganized sector, and those without sons or children have to be looked after by the state. One needs to estimate their numbers to assess the funds necessary for looking after them.

The examination of the life-cycle in India reveals that in the mid-fifties the old died before taking care of their responsibilities. Things improved considerably by 1990; but without proper education, the desired goals of a responsibility-free old age could not be attained as shown by the 1990 life-cycle. Thus a problem-free old age is possible only with a small number of educated children who can not only look after themselves, but also after their parents.

Work participation rates are higher in old age but they speak more for the shortage of necessities experienced by the old. With better industrialization and better levels of living, one expects the work participation rates in old age to fall.

Poverty in old age is a universal problem, observed even in rich countries like the United States. The reasons for this are inflation and expenditure on medicine and health. But in India poverty in old age is just a hangover of the condition of younger years. The dependency load on the young increases with old age and is more so among the poor than the better off as seen in some surveys. There is a need for social security but this hardly exists for a vast section of the population in India. This is the crux of the problem. How is the government or any other agency going to handle it?

3

Interstate Variations in the Old

Though we were specifically interested in the aged population of Maharashtra, we wished to compare the conditions of the old in various states of the country. Did they differ much? If so, was the difference due to the socio-cultural diversity of the states? If the variations were insignificant, why was this so? Were poverty and dependence on agriculture the overwhelming common factors which made the states very similar in their aged populations? Such questions needed an answer. For this purpose statewise pictures of the old were required. To get representative samples of the old in various states was a costly affair. But this need was fortunately satisfied by the 42nd round of the National Sample Survey Organization (NSSO) described below.

At the instance of the Ministry of Social Welfare, the NSSO conducted a nationwide survey to assess the nature and dimensions of the socio-economic problems of the old, i.e., persons of 60 years and above, in its 42nd round from July 1986 to June 1987. The survey covered the whole of the Indian Union except the Ladakh and Kargil districts of Jammu and Kashmir and the rural areas of Nagaland.

For such a countrywide survey it was necessary to select a representative sample of old men and women. The sampling procedure adopted for the survey was a two-stage stratified design. The first-stage units were villages in the rural sector and blocks from the urban frame of the survey of the NSSO. The second-stage units were households in both the sectors.

For selection of the sample households, the frame consisted of households having at least one member aged 60 years and above. The survey covered about 50,000 households spread over a sample of 8,312 villages and 4,446 urban blocks in the country. The number of households surveyed in the rural and urban areas in each state is set out in Table 3.1. It gives an idea as to the spread of enquiry in the various states of the country into the socio-economic and demographic conditions of the old.

Table 3.1
Number of Households Surveyed in Rural and Urban Areas of Various States

State	Rural	Urban	Total
Andhra Pradesh	2,448	1,340	3,788
Assam	1,440	467	1,907
Bihar	3,123	805	3,928
Gujarat	1,117	900	2,017
Haryana	438	232	670
Himachal Pradesh	739	166	905
Jammu & Kashmir	1,187	569	1,756
Karnataka	1,359	913	2,272
Kerala	1,240	511	1,751
Madhya Pradesh	2,519	1,182	3,701
Maharashtra	2,248	2,118	4,366
Orissa	1,410	463	1,873
Punjab	893	695	1,588
Rajasthan	1,418	673	2,091
Tamil Nadu	1,865	1,655	3,520
Uttar Pradesh	4,040	1,754	5,794
West Bengal	1,987	1,317	3,304
All India	32,237	17,456	49,693

Source: For all tables in this chapter, 42nd Round of the National Sample Survey Report, unless specified otherwise.

A total of 49,693 households were actually surveyed in India as a whole. From Maharashtra 4,366 households were surveyed. Thus, the enquiry covered a large number of households, representing the population of the old in various states. Table 3.2. shows the projected population aged 60 years and above in rural and urban areas of various states for January 1987. In all, we will be looking at 48,712,300 old men and women in India.

Table 3.2
Projected Population (in Hundreds) of Age 60 Years and Above by Sex as on 1st January 1987 for Rural and Urban Sectors of Selected States and All-India

State (1)	Rural				Urban			
	Male (2)	Female (3)	All (4)	Sex Ratio (5)	Male (6)	Female (7)	All (8)	Sex Ratio (9)
Andhra Pradesh	16,720	16,179	32,899	968	3,889	4,285	8,174	1,102
Assam	4,948	3,571	8,519	721	496	402	898	810
Bihar	23,048	20,750	43,798	900	2,639	2,430	5,069	921
Gujarat	7,970	8,162	16,132	1,024	3,091	3,319	6,410	1,096
Haryana	4,244	3,085	7,329	727	1,091	1,015	2,106	930
Himachal Pradesh	2,086	1,669	3,755	800	122	87	209	713
Jammu and Kashmir	1,989	1,285	3,274	646	381	322	703	841
Karnataka	9,967	9,595	19,562	963	3,633	3,866	7,499	1,064
Kerala	8,308	9,426	17,734	1,135	1,853	2,393	4,246	1,291
Madhya Pradesh	13,436	14,944	28,380	1,112	3,044	3,258	6,302	1,070
Maharashtra	16,526	16,766	33,292	1,015	7,108	7,008	14,116	985
Orissa	8,339	8,173	16,512	980	951	978	1,929	1,028
Punjab	6,177	5,042	11,219	816	1,829	1,621	3,450	886
Rajasthan	9,100	8,568	17,668	942	2,218	2,308	4,526	1,041
Tamil Nadu	13,824	12,306	26,130	890	5,872	5,992	11,864	1,020
Uttar Pradesh	35,141	29,943	65,084	852	7,027	5,950	12,977	847
West Bengal	12,517	12,068	24,585	964	5,191	4,378	9,569	843
All India	195,828	188,049	383,877	960	51,466	51,780	103,246	1,006

Source: Expert Committee Report on Population Projections for India up to 2001 (1980).

The sex-ratio of the old for the country as a whole was 970 females per 1000 males, which is quite disproportionate to what one finds in the rest of the world. However, it may be noted that the sex ratio was more unequal for all ages put together, and the 970 females per 1000 males was perhaps the improved figure for old age.

In rural areas only the four states of Kerala, MP, Gujarat and Maharashtra had a favourable female/male sex ratio. Jammu and Kashmir, Assam and Haryana had the most unfavourable sex ratio in that order. This is unusual for India where women do not migrate to urban areas without their menfolk. Moreover the small numbers of females in rural areas was not compensated for by their greater numbers in urban areas. Thus, unfavourable female/male sex ratios in a larger number of states could possibly be caused by their higher mortality in rural areas. As noted throughout this chapter, women always suffered from poorer health as compared to men. This was not found elsewhere, at least in the advanced world, where men were always fewer in numbers in old age compared to women. One may venture to conclude that sociological factors proved predominant in India, overriding the biological superiority of females observed elsewhere. Probably it was the low status of the females that explained these small numbers. Women perhaps had higher mortality than men. As for urban areas, conditions were better and perhaps the mortality among women was also relatively small as judged from the sex ratios presented in Table 3.2.

Living Arrangements

Were Elderly Men and Women Lonely?

One of the curses of old age is to be forced to live alone without anybody around to look after one. The percentage of such lonely ones in rural and urban areas is revealed in Table 3.3 for the various states of the country.

The total reveals that 12 per cent of the aged men and a little over 1 per cent of women were living alone in rural areas. In urban areas 9.5 per cent of men and 0.8 per cent of women lived alone. It is difficult to explain why so many more men than women lived

Table 3.3
Percentage of Old Men and Women Living Alone in Rural and Urban Areas of Various States

State	Rural		Urban	
	Men	Women	Men	Women
Andhra Pradesh	14.9	0.6	11.3	0.8
Assam	5.6	2.6	8.2	6.8
Bihar	10.6	1.1	8.6	0.2
Gujarat	14.7	1.5	15.7	1.5
Haryana	5.6	–	12.7	1.7
Himachal Pradesh	12.6	1.9	16.4	–
Jammu and Kashmir	5.3	0.7	6.3	2.0
Karnataka	9.5	0.6	7.8	–
Kerala	6.2	1.5	7.1	0.8
Madhya Pradesh	14.4	1.7	9.0	0.7
Maharashtra	12.0	0.3	8.7	0.8
Orissa	14.3	1.1	8.3	0.4
Punjab	7.2	0.5	10.4	1.2
Rajasthan	8.6	1.4	10.9	0.2
Tamil Nadu	4.7	3.1	6.9	–
Uttar Pradesh	17.0	1.2	10.7	1.1
West Bengal	9.6	1.3	6.1	0.1
All India	12.4	1.4	9.5	0.8

alone. Probably, women when alone prefer to find some companionship, which men do not do to the same extent. However, in the Western world more women live alone.

If the problems of the old are to be tackled, one has to concentrate more on the problems of lonely men than women.

How Many Elderly Men and Women Were Living Without (a) A Surviving Son or (b) Without a Son or A Daughter in Rural and Urban Areas?

This was a very pertinent question to ask because in many states the old-age pension was given to those who had no adult son or daughter. Thus from the percentage of (a) (refer to above heading) one can arrive at the percentage of old who qualified for getting old-age pension in the state. The data for the country as a whole and the various states are presented in Tables 3.4 and 3.5.

Table 3.4
Percentage Distribution of Persons by Sex, Age and Number of Surviving Sons and Daughters for Rural and Urban Sectors of India

Sex (1)	Age (2)	Number of Surviving Sons and Daughters					
		No Child Born Alive (3)	At Least One Son but No Daughter (4)	At Least One Daughter but No Son (5)	At Least One Son and One Daughter (6)	No Surviving Son and Daughter (7)	All types (8)
		Rural					
Male	60–64	4.31	11.99	9.24	72.21	2.25	100.00
	65–69	5.35	12.11	9.27	70.56	2.72	100.00
	70 & above	5.19	12.41	7.74	71.77	2.90	100.00
	60 & above	4.86	12.15	8.80	71.61	2.58	100.00
Female	60–64	3.64	14.68	5.89	74.18	1.62	100.00
	65–69	3.35	15.12	6.35	72.88	2.30	100.00
	70 & above	3.63	15.97	7.29	70.66	2.44	100.00
	60 & above	3.56	15.19	6.44	72.75	2.06	100.00
Persons	60–64	4.04	13.07	7.89	73.00	2.00	100.00
	65–69	4.55	13.32	8.09	71.49	2.55	100.00
	70 & above	4.56	13.85	7.56	71.32	2.71	100.00
	60 & above	4.34	13.37	7.85	72.07	2.37	100.00

Male	60–64	4.31	11.22	6.41	75.03	3.03	100.00
	65–69	5.60	10.94	8.42	71.89	3.14	100.00
	70 & above	6.01	11.86	7.78	71.20	3.15	100.00
	60 & above	5.22	11.35	7.41	72.92	3.10	100.00
Female	60–64	4.96	14.14	6.51	72.21	2.18	100.00
	65–69	3.68	13.55	7.23	72.50	3.04	100.00
	70 & above	4.25	16.33	7.17	69.83	2.43	100.00
	60 & above	4.35	14.75	6.95	71.45	2.57	100.00
Persons	60–64	4.56	12.36	6.45	73.93	2.70	100.00
	65–69	4.81	12.01	7.93	72.14	3.10	100.00
	70 & above	5.25	13.80	7.51	70.61	2.83	100.00
	60 & above	4.86	12.75	7.22	72.31	2.86	100.00

Table 3.5
**Old Persons in Rural and Urban Areas of Various States Having
(a) No Sons and (b) Neither Sons Nor Daughters**

	No Sons (a)		Neither Sons Nor Daughters (b)	
	Rural	Urban	Rural	Urban
All India	14.56	14.94	6.71	7.72
Andhra Pradesh	18.65	18.28	7.40	8.72
Assam	4.65	9.26	3.12	6.02
Bihar	13.28	13.34	7.01	7.43
Gujarat	11.25	13.22	5.25	7.33
Haryana	10.35	14.66	4.32	7.66
Himachal Pradesh	17.35	12.39	10.50	9.36
Jammu & Kashmir	15.36	10.56	7.90	5.14
Karnataka	14.93	13.64	6.38	8.45
Kerala	13.71	16.77	4.59	9.92
Madhya Pradesh	19.50	11.76	10.45	6.47
Maharashtra	15.63	15.94	6.61	7.57
Orissa	15.63	12.79	7.14	6.20
Punjab	10.04	12.23	5.80	6.12
Rajasthan	11.50	12.21	6.02	7.25
Tamil Nadu	18.63	19.22	7.76	9.41
Uttar Pradesh	14.22	14.82	7.73	7.65
West Bengal	13.24	14.59	5.85	7.39

In the country as a whole about 15 per cent had no son in rural or urban areas. Thus they deserved an old-age pension if other conditions were satisfied. There were 8 per cent who had neither a son nor a daughter. If they got bedridden, in old age, they would be left helpless in the absence of state assistance.

Among the various states MP, AP and Tamil Nadu had the largest percentages having no son in rural areas. Tamil Nadu and AP had the largest percentages even in urban areas. Among those having neither son nor daughter Assam had the lowest percentage in rural areas and Himachal Pradesh the highest. Otherwise, the difference from state to state was little. Even for Himachal Pradesh, our feeling is that this state had a smaller sample and hence a larger variation when compared to the other states.

How Many Old Men Were Economically Independent? How Many Were Totally Dependent on Others? Had Those Among the Economically Independent any Dependency Load?

Answers to these questions can be found for men in Table 3.6 which also throws light on the conditions of the old in India and the various states. In India as a whole 51 per cent of men in rural and 46 per cent in urban areas were economically independent. Of these about 71 per cent, both in rural and urban areas, had to carry a load of dependency. In other words, the independent men were still working and were not yet free of responsibilities. Many of them had worked all their lives at a level of earning where they could save very little for their old age. That is why this chain of the old carrying responsibility followed by their total dependence on

Table 3.6
Percentage of Economically Independent Men and Totally Dependent Men in Rural and Urban Areas of States and the Percentage of Independent Men Carrying a Dependency Load Even in Old Age

State	Independent		Totally Dependent		Independents Carrying Dependency Load	
	Rural	Urban	Rural	Urban	Rural	Urban
All India	51.1	45.7	32.7	37.4	70.7	71.6
AP	54.4	50.7	34.4	35.3	74.9	72.0
Assam	35.2	35.6	43.9	42.0	88.1	83.8
Bihar	47.9	45.6	32.6	38.9	63.6	70.3
Gujarat	43.1	38.2	39.1	46.8	65.2	57.6
Haryana	43.5	39.4	48.3	44.1	82.3	76.0
HP	59.4	59.9	25.1	28.6	68.4	58.7
J & K	59.3	53.0	24.0	28.0	77.3	80.4
Karnataka	46.3	42.0	46.0	38.3	57.4	77.9
Kerala	46.3	39.4	41.0	46.8	78.2	79.4
MP	55.5	49.6	31.1	33.9	67.2	69.8
Maharashtra	47.4	43.6	38.3	32.7	63.7	66.4
Orissa	42.6	33.4	37.5	39.2	64.3	61.5
Punjab	48.2	48.6	42.3	41.8	78.8	71.1
Rajasthan	41.3	41.7	38.8	37.2	62.3	61.3
Tamil Nadu	50.3	44.7	31.1	32.7	70.4	73.7
UP	55.1	51.6	27.2	34.6	65.6	73.7
West Bengal	44.0	50.0	39.7	35.7	76.2	79.5

their own children had to continue. One-third or more in rural and urban areas were totally dependent on others.

Jammu and Kashmir and Himachal Pradesh had the smallest percentage of totally dependent men. At the other extreme were rural Haryana and Karnataka where the totally dependent old were only a little less than 50 per cent. Among the independent men in rural Assam, 88 per cent reported having a load of dependency. It is also possible that rural men with land to work on reported that they had to carry a load of dependency, not accounting for the fact that others in the household also worked equally hard. As these men were assumed to hold the headship, their reports were solicited. On the whole however, young and old had to work hard and help each other.

A positive observation from Table 3.6 is that economically the men, even when old, were integrated with the economic life of the community, and thus large numbers were not isolated as they would have been if they had to retire.

For India as a whole more details are given in Table 3.7 regarding the degree of economic dependence of men and women by age groups. One can see from this table how the dependence of men increases rapidly with age, especially after the age of 70.

As for women, they were economically independent in a very small percentage of cases, and that too decreased with age. Data for both men and women in Maharashtra are shown in Table 3.8.

What can be noted is that the conditions in Maharashtra closely resemble those for an all-India average. Whatever little variation observed can be explained by the sampling variation. Hence our idea was to present the details of data for India as a whole and not to repeat these for Maharashtra unless they differ significantly from average India.

As can be seen from Table 3.8, 38 per cent rural and 33 per cent urban men had to be totally supported by others. As for women, 82 per cent in rural areas and 88 per cent in urban areas had to be fully supported by others. The question then was: Who supported them?

Support for Elderly Men and Women

As Table 3.9 shows, National Sample Survey classified those providing support to the old as: (*i*) spouse (*ii*) own children (*iii*)

Table 3.7
Percentage Distribution of Persons by Sex, Age and Degree of Economic Independence and Percentage of Persons with Dependents Among Economically Independent Persons for Rural and Urban Sectors, All-India

Sex	Age	Degree of Economic Independence				Per Cent with Dependents Among Economically Independent
		Not Dependent on Others	Partially Dependent on Others	Fully Dependent on Others	All Types	
(1)	(2)	(3)	(4)	(5)	(6)	(7)
		Rural				
Male	60–64	63.91	15.41	20.68	100.00	76.32
	65–69	51.43	18.01	30.56	100.00	69.63
	70 & above	32.86	15.62	51.53	100.00	57.08
	60 & above	51.06	16.20	32.74	100.00	70.71
Female	60–64	14.26	18.87	66.87	100.00	53.12
	65–69	6.90	12.87	80.23	100.00	47.36
	70 & above	2.99	7.40	89.61	100.00	43.16
	60 & above	8.78	13.71	77.51	100.00	50.83
Persons	60–64	43.96	16.80	39.24	100.00	73.29
	65–69	33.51	15.95	50.54	100.00	67.78
	70 & above	20.75	12.29	66.97	100.00	56.27
	60 & above	34.02	15.20	50.78	100.00	68.64
		Urban				
Male	60–64	56.74	15.80	27.46	100.00	78.21
	65–69	47.58	18.47	33.95	100.00	69.22
	70 & above	30.55	16.89	52.56	100.00	59.93
	60 & above	45.71	16.90	37.39	100.00	71.64
Female	60–64	6.81	12.39	80.80	100.00	35.33
	65–69	5.09	10.10	84.81	100.00	40.52
	70 & above	2.60	4.99	92.41	100.00	28.81
	60 & above	4.84	9.13	86.04	100.00	35.61
Persons	60–64	37.24	14.47	48.29	100.00	75.14
	65–69	30.16	15.04	54.80	100.00	67.24
	70 & above	18.45	11.74	69.81	100.00	58.03
	60 & above	28.94	13.71	57.35	100.00	69.17

Table 3.8
Percentage Distribution of Persons by Sex, Age and Degree of Economic Independence and Percentage of Persons with Dependents Among Economically Independent Persons for Rural and Urban Sectors of Maharashtra

Sex	Age	Degree of Economic Independence				Per Cent with Dependents Among Economically Independent
		Not Dependent on Others	Partially Dependent on Others	Fully Dependent on Others	All Types	
(1)	(2)	(3)	(4)	(5)	(6)	(7)
		Rural				
Male	60–64	53.36	17.98	24.66	100.00	69.83
	65–69	51.74	14.33	33.92	100.00	62.51
	70 & above	31.21	9.92	58.87	100.00	52.68
	60 & above	47.44	14.29	38.27	100.00	63.71
Female	60–64	11.28	14.13	74.59	100.00	26.85
	65–69	7.03	11.46	81.51	100.00	20.89
	70 & above	2.84	6.45	90.71	100.00	53.00
	60 & above	7.43	11.00	81.57	100.00	28.08
Persons	60–64	36.63	16.25	47.11	100.00	63.88
	65–69	33.13	13.14	53.74	100.00	58.83
	70 & above	19.18	8.45	72.37	100.00	52.70
	60 & above	30.19	12.87	56.94	100.00	59.93
		Urban				
Male	60–64	52.96	19.66	27.38	100.00	73.84
	65–69	48.13	18.60	33.27	100.00	60.57
	70 & above	28.70	20.81	50.49	100.00	59.40
	60 & above	47.58	19.73	32.69	100.00	66.42
Female	60–64	5.32	9.69	84.99	100.00	55.63
	65–69	6.33	7.50	86.17	100.00	12.97
	70 & above	2.68	3.99	93.33	100.00	25.59
	60 & above	4.66	7.08	88.26	100.00	33.75
Persons	60–64	32.70	15.42	51.88	100.00	72.58
	65–69	31.01	14.06	54.93	100.00	56.59
	70 & above	17.07	13.29	69.64	100.00	57.03
	60 & above	26.92	14.31	58.77	100.00	64.00

grandchildren and (*iv*) others. Roughly 7 per cent of men and about 11 per cent of women were supported by their spouses. Approximately three-fourths were supported by their own children. About 6 per cent were supported by their grandchildren. Eight to twelve per cent of men and women were supported by others. It was this last category that needed government or public support. One wondered whether support or help from society would be preferable to government assistance. As will be seen in Chapter 5, villagers did not like the idea of seeking help from the government—they called it 'begging'. They preferred to approach villagers known to them for help. The relevant data regarding support of elderly men and women for India as a whole and for the various states are set out in Tables 3.9 and 3.10 respectively.

Table 3.9
Percentage Distribution of the Old in India in Rural and Urban Areas According to the Category of Persons Supporting Them

	Age Group		Spouse	Own Children	Grand-children	Others	All Categories
Males	60+	Rural	7.04	74.95	6.24	11.78	100
		Urban	6.14	78.03	6.11	9.72	100
Females	60+	Rural	11.51	73.84	6.38	8.27	100
		Urban	11.30	72.32	6.52	9.86	100

As seen in Table 3.10, the pattern of support of the old was more or less the same in many states. Only Assam and Himachal Pradesh showed some extreme observations. For instance in urban Assam, the smallest number (3.56 per cent) were supported by spouses, while urban Himachal Pradesh was at the other extreme, i.e., 20 per cent spouses supporting their old partners. This could perhaps be explained by the smallness of sample of that state or the living conditions being different there. Moreover, Assam, Himachal Pradesh or Jammu and Kashmir are very mountainous and their economies differ from those of other states. Otherwise most of the states showed about 9 per cent of the old supported by their spouses, three-fourths supported by children and 6 per cent supported by grandchildren. 'Others' supported the old in 10 to 12 per cent cases in many states, and some variations from the average could be explained by the size of sampling.

Table 3.10

Pattern of Support of Old Persons Above 60 Years of Age in Various States in Rural and Urban Areas

State		Spouse	Own Children	Grand-children	Others	All Categories
All India	R	9.53	74.33	6.32	9.82	100
	U	8.98	74.89	6.33	9.80	100
Andhra Pradesh	R	9.55	70.52	6.59	13.34	100
	U	7.31	73.65	7.61	11.42	100
Assam	R	4.21	87.01	5.61	3.17	100
	U	3.56	76.59	7.92	11.93	100
Bihar	R	8.62	77.01	6.80	8.06	100
	U	9.97	75.23	7.00	7.80	100
Gujarat	R	9.31	79.11	6.38	5.19	100
	U	5.09	81.62	7.50	5.78	100
Haryana	R	10.52	78.74	4.22	6.52	100
	U	8.23	71.82	4.21	15.74	100
Himachal Pradesh	R	9.26	75.74	3.68	11.32	100
	U	20.20	65.69	6.11	7.68	100
Jammu & Kashmir	R	11.39	73.52	4.18	10.90	100
	U	9.27	78.73	4.67	7.33	100
Karnataka	R	9.70	73.49	7.24	9.57	100
	U	6.83	78.33	5.95	8.89	100
Kerala	R	12.36	70.68	7.64	9.32	100
	U	6.00	73.53	5.75	14.72	100
Madhya Pradesh	R	8.42	69.87	10.83	10.88	100
	U	9.49	74.50	8.18	7.84	100
Maharashtra	R	8.81	74.54	5.83	10.82	100
	U	9.47	74.65	6.88	9.01	100
Orissa	R	10.03	74.63	6.41	8.93	100
	U	9.20	82.07	3.27	5.46	100
Punjab	R	11.99	74.72	3.98	9.32	100
	U	12.83	75.19	4.21	7.77	100
Rajasthan	R	6.45	79.38	7.34	6.83	100
	U	6.22	77.53	5.10	11.15	100
Tamil Nadu	R	13.51	71.28	4.82	10.40	100
	U	10.12	73.31	5.55	11.01	100
Uttar Pradesh	R	9.98	74.11	6.50	9.40	100
	U	10.87	72.68	5.83	10.62	100
West Bengal	R	9.08	73.53	6.03	11.36	100
	U	9.35	72.96	6.44	11.25	100

With Whom did the Elderly Live?

The old were classified according to the persons they lived with. For instance, they could live alone as an inmate of an old-age home or live alone but not in such a home. They could live with spouses or children or grandchildren. They could also live with other relatives, even distant ones or with non-relations. Their percentages in different categories are set out in Table 3.11 for the country as a whole for rural and urban areas, and for males and females separately in various age groups of the old.

In rural and urban India, respectively, 6.8 and 4 persons per 1000 lived in old-age homes. This meant that roughly 261,000 persons from rural areas and 41,000 from urban areas lived in old-age homes in India. In others words, only about 300,000 people lived in old-age homes in the country as a whole. This is not surprising since nowhere did the old prefer living in old-age homes away from their own homes. Moreover, in India the increase in longevity is a recent phenomenon and very little has been done by the government or voluntary agencies to promote the running of old-age homes. Even in the advanced countries of the West, living in old-age homes was not popular. For instance, in the United States where the longevity is much higher and government or voluntary agencies take ample care of the old, the percentage of those living in old-age homes was only 10 times that in India— namely, about 5 per cent (see Table 2.14 in Chapter II).

Returning to the situation in India, seven per cent lived alone in rural areas and about five and a half per cent in urban areas. Those living alone and those living with 'other' relations or non-relations formed about 11 per cent or so. These were the ones that seemed most in need of support—they could be called *niradhar*, as the term goes in Maharashtra. One may note here that the Sanjay Niradhar Anudan Yojana (SNAY), a kind of old-age pension scheme in Maharashtra, described later in this report, is aimed at such people.

About half the old lived with children and more than one-third lived with spouses. Thus more than 85 per cent had close supporters to take care of them. In Chapter Two percentages of the old living with children were noted for Britain, USA and Denmark. It was found that 42 per cent in Britain, 28 per cent in the USA and 20 per cent in Denmark lived with their children, and a sizeable

Table 3.11
Percentage Distribution of Persons by Sex, Age and Living Arrangements for Rural and Urban Sectors of India

Sex (1)	Age (2)	Living Arrangement Code*							
		0 (3)	1 (4)	2 (5)	3 (6)	4 (7)	5 (8)	6 (9)	All (10)
				Rural					
Male	60-64	0.49	10.87	49.70	34.45	1.63	2.53	0.28	100.00
	65-69	0.87	11.67	45.74	35.81	2.12	3.52	0.26	100.00
	70 & above	0.67	13.14	37.87	41.06	2.83	3.96	0.48	100.00
	60 & above	0.65	11.78	45.00	36.82	2.13	3.24	0.33	100.00
Female	60-64	1.25	0.78	33.61	59.49	1.34	3.33	0.22	100.00
	65-69	0.53	0.66	25.11	66.44	2.18	5.01	0.09	100.00
	70 & above	0.22	0.59	13.31	74.43	5.17	6.13	0.15	100.00
	60 & above	0.74	0.69	25.06	65.97	2.74	4.65	0.16	100.00
Persons	60-64	0.79	6.82	43.27	44.50	1.51	2.85	0.25	100.00
	65-69	0.74	7.24	37.44	48.13	2.14	4.12	0.19	100.00
	70 & above	0.49	8.05	27.91	54.59	3.78	4.84	0.35	100.00
	60 & above	0.68	7.31	37.00	48.57	2.37	3.81	0.25	100.00

Urban

		0	1	2	3	4	5	6	
Male	60–64	0.33	8.24	48.78	37.86	1.16	3.17	0.46	100.00
	65–69	0.72	9.70	47.83	35.80	2.16	3.42	0.38	100.00
	70 & above	0.66	9.28	37.49	45.07	2.64	4.53	0.34	100.00
	60 & above	0.54	8.98	44.87	39.61	1.92	3.68	0.40	100.00
Female	60–64	0.29	0.68	30.31	61.70	1.69	5.17	0.18	100.00
	65–69	0.14	0.67	22.28	66.51	2.17	7.60	0.63	100.00
	70 & above	0.16	0.46	11.74	73.63	5.03	8.44	0.53	100.00
	60 & above	0.20	0.60	21.47	67.28	3.01	7.01	0.43	100.00
Persons	60–64	0.31	5.29	41.57	47.16	1.37	3.95	0.35	100.00
	65–69	0.48	5.99	37.33	48.42	2.16	5.14	0.48	100.00
	70 & above	0.44	5.45	26.32	57.46	3.68	6.23	0.42	100.00
	60 & above	0.40	5.54	35.26	50.97	2.37	5.05	0.41	100.00

* Living Arrangement Code: 0 – Living alone as an inmate of home for aged persons.
1 – Living alone but not as an inmate of home for aged persons.
2 – Living with spouse.
3 – Living with own children.
4 – Living with grandchildren.
5 – Living with other relations.
6 – Living with non-relations.

percentage had children living at a distance which could be covered in ten minutes or less (see Table 2.12). Thus living arrangements in India and these countries seem different only because of economic circumstances. In India the parents and grown-up children could not afford to have separate accommodation. But as far as the proximity of spouses and children was concerned, these countries did not appear very different from India.

Where children and parents lived together, help of any kind (such as economic, emotional, household management, child care, illness) received or given by the old could not be finely classified. But the data in Table 3.12 classified for the United States correspond closely with the Indian expectation regarding the old and their grown-up children and again emphasizes the fact that the basic needs of the old everywhere are more or less the same.

From Table 3.12 it can be seen that the maximum economic help was given by parents and received by married children and grandparents in that order. Emotional gratification was given most by the parents and received most by grandparents. The same was true of household management. Child care was given most by parents and received most by married children. In illness, married children gave most help and grandparents received the most. In short, among the three generations the middle generation of parents gave the most, both to the younger and older generation. This sort of give and take seemed natural, the youngest generation helping the most in illness.

What is most noticeable in Table 3.13 is the more or less uniformity in the living arrangements of the old across various states, disturbed only by sampling variations. This is not surprising since the lifestyle of the people—a complex product of the economic, social and cultural milieu—does not differ much from state to state. Living in old-age homes is not approved of in the Indian culture, nor are people used to the idea since it is a comparatively recent phenomenon and necessary arrangements are not readily available. The concept of the old-age home has not yet reached the rural areas; hence even in the few old-age homes which exist in India, the inhabitants come from cities and urban areas rather than villages. To run old-age homes, governments and voluntary agencies have to come forward extensively. In the United States the growth of old-age homes was fuelled by the profitability of the business. There are many lonely and helpless old in India who have nowhere

Table 3.12

Comparison of Help Received and Help Given by Different Generations for Chief Problem Areas (Percentages)

Generation	Types of Crisis									
	Economic		Emotional Gratification		Household Management		Child Care		Illness Care	
	Gave	Received	Gave	Received	Gave	Received	Gave	Received	Gave	Received
Grand parents	26	34	23	42	21	52	16	0	32	61
Parents	41	17	47	37	47	23	50	23	21	21
Married children	34	49	31	21	33	25	34	78	47	18

Source: Hill (1965).

Table 3.13

Living Arrangement of Old Persons in Various States

States		Old-age Home	Alone	With Spouse	With Own Children	With Grand-children	Other Relations	Not With Relations	All
Andhra Pradesh	R	0.93	8.78	38.79	42.53	3.10	5.77	0.11	100
	U	0.77	5.56	32.98	49.14	4.29	6.72	0.54	100
Assam	R	1.81	2.73	27.51	66.09	0.40	1.28	0.17	100
	U	4.09	3.59	26.35	60.75	0.71	4.50	–	100
Bihar	R	0.52	5.91	25.88	60.35	3.76	3.43	0.14	100
	U	0.06	4.99	23.06	63.55	3.02	4.72	0.60	100
Gujarat	R	1.05	7.60	40.37	47.67	1.66	1.65	–	100
	U	1.46	8.03	30.28	35.18	2.44	2.61	–	100
Haryana	R	0.27	3.38	50.86	40.09	2.58	2.82	–	100
	U	0.16	7.96	40.01	42.29	2.53	7.04	–	100
Himachal Pradesh	R	0.11	9.34	30.23	52.62	2.54	5.11	0.06	100
	U	0.09	11.19	31.11	52.27	1.03	3.60	0.71	100
Jammu & Kashmir	R	0.34	3.33	51.13	38.21	1.24	5.45	0.31	100
	U	0.94	3.96	49.60	41.01	0.93	3.26	0.28	100
Karnataka	R	0.52	5.56	38.49	47.88	2.71	4.62	0.23	100
	U	0.42	4.28	38.07	50.28	1.97	4.73	0.25	100
Kerala	R	0.33	4.43	48.34	40.40	1.56	3.55	1.39	100
	U	1.27	3.49	37.94	46.21	1.37	9.62	0.11	100
Madhya Pradesh	R	0.71	8.13	34.30	48.88	3.14	4.40	0.44	100
	U	0.27	5.04	32.10	57.15	2.71	2.56	0.17	100
Maharashtra	R	0.29	6.66	42.12	43.80	2.54	4.28	0.30	100
	U	0.12	5.22	33.26	54.71	1.59	4.59	0.51	100

Orissa	R	0.71	7.69	36.68	49.65	1.80	3.10	0.37	100
	U	0.50	4.41	28.88	61.45	1.36	3.34	0.04	100
Punjab	R	0.31	4.49	50.42	38.48	1.10	4.70	0.50	100
	U	0.38	6.61	47.76	38.86	1.37	4.92	0.09	100
Rajasthan	R	0.48	4.67	27.50	61.40	2.22	3.59	0.13	100
	U	–	6.12	25.27	61.14	2.01	4.48	0.47	100
Tamil Nadu	R	0.28	11.22	46.52	35.19	2.36	4.29	0.14	100
	U	0.11	5.48	39.31	45.20	2.40	6.89	0.61	100
Uttar Pradesh	R	0.41	10.13	31.34	51.74	2.05	4.09	0.24	100
	U	0.21	6.79	36.51	48.08	3.91	4.14	0.35	100
West Bengal	R	0.60	5.51	38.68	49.03	2.38	3.47	0.33	100
	U	0.11	3.82	39.89	48.44	1.27	5.61	0.86	100
All India	R	0.68	7.31	37.00	48.57	2.37	3.81	0.25	100
	U	0.40	5.54	35.26	50.97	2.37	5.05	0.41	100

to go. Most of the old from among households living below the poverty line can be helped in their own homes with old-age pensions because this would be cheaper to provide and more preferable to the old. In fact the Sanjay Niradhar Yojana in Maharashtra was started in 1980 on this very basis. This is described in a later chapter.

As seen in Table 3.13, Assam, followed by Gujarat, had a relatively larger percentage of persons living in old-age homes, particularly urban Assam, having 4 per cent, which came close to that of the United States' 5 per cent living in old-age homes (Ward, 1979: 50). It is pertinent to ask why urban Assam had more old-age homes. Our guess is that it was partly explained by the influence of tribal culture in the Assam hills and of Christianity.

Living alone varied from about 2 per cent to 11 per cent, both the extremes being observable in the rural and urban areas of Himachal Pradesh. The peculiarity of Himachal Pradesh is that it is a fruit-growing state as well as a mountainous one, but that alone does not explain the extreme observations. Rural Tamil Nadu also had a large percentage (11 per cent) living alone.

Urban Kerala had the highest percentage, i.e. 9.62, of old living with other relations. It is not unlikely that their children had migrated for employment, leaving their old with other relations.

Health and Mobility

What Percentage of Men and Women Were Immobile in Old Age?

One of the curses of old age is immobility due to illness or disease. About 5 per cent of the old persons in rural and urban areas of India (about 4 per cent men and 7 per cent women) were physically immobile. Relevant data for rural and urban India for the two sexes separately and combined are presented in Table 3.14. Women were more immobile than men. One wondered why it was that women who are biologically stronger and live longer were weaker in India. Was it the burden of childbearing without nutrition? Was it her low status in the family which kept her less fed?

In Table 3.14 the separate and combined figures for immobile men and women are displayed by age groups. One has to note that more than half or a little less than 60 per cent of the immobile in rural and urban areas were from the age group 70+.

Table 3.14 also presents the data for answering the following questions

Since the Immobile Had to be Helped. Who was Helping Them? Was it Men or Women?

Among those who had to help the immobile, about 92 per cent were household members. About 7 per cent were other than household members. It would be interesting to know who comprised this latter group. As for the household members, it was no surprise that female members looked after the immobile in larger numbers, more so in urban areas. What was pleasantly surprising was that 30/35 per cent of male household members also looked after the immobile in urban/rural areas. All these data are presented in Table 3.14 for the country as a whole.

In Table 3.15 the percentages of immobile men and women in various major states of the country are exhibited for rural and urban areas. These groups of men and women always suffer the most anywhere in the world. Invariably in India, the percentage of immobile women compared to men is larger with the exception of rural Haryana which is an agriculturally advanced state. In rural areas of Karnataka and West Bengal and urban areas of Orissa and West Bengal the percentage of immobile women was 10 or more. It could be that in these regions people suffered from chronic diseases.

How Many Among the Elderly Were Chronically Ill? And What Kinds of Diseases Were They Suffering From?

Old men and women in rural and urban areas were asked about their chronic complaints and the relevant data are presented in Table 3.16. In column 3 of the table, the percentage of the chronically ill is given for rural and urban areas for males and females in various age groups.

As expected the percentage of chronically ill increased with age. One has to remember that these were only chronic complaints and not necessarily serious, disabling illnesses. The percentage of those ill was about 39 among males and females in the age group 60–64

Table 3.14
Percentage of Physically Immovable Persons in Different Age Groups and Their Percentage Distribution Over Age, and Percentage Distribution of Physically Immovable Persons Helped by Household Members and Others

				Percentage Distribution of Immobile Persons According to Category of Help			
				Household Member		Other than Household Member	
Sex	Age	Proportion of Physically Immobile Persons	Distribution of Physically Immobile Persons	Male	Female	Male	Female
(1)	(2)	(3)	(4)	(5)	(6)	(7)	(8)
			Rural				
Male	60–64	2.404	22.71	46.08	48.24	3.78	1.90
	65–69	3.332	20.88	45.95	44.91	6.29	2.85
	70 & above	8.326	56.41	42.08	46.46	8.13	3.33
	60 & above	4.447	100.00	43.77	46.52	6.80	2.92
Female	60–64	3.251	19.93	34.31	57.19	4.48	4.02
	65–69	4.871	19.88	34.20	59.90	1.95	3.95
	70 & above	13.457	60.19	26.76	68.67	2.38	2.19
	60 & above	6.809	100.00	29.69	64.69	2.72	2.89
Persons	60–64	2.744	21.30	40.26	52.67	4.13	2.94
	65–69	3.951	20.37	40.21	52.23	4.17	3.39
	70 & above	10.407	58.33	33.96	58.24	5.08	2.72
	60 & above	5.399	100.00	36.53	55.87	4.70	2.90

Urban

Male						
60–64	2.236	19.10	28.05	61.19	7.20	3.56
65–69	4.111	24.66	31.56	59.36	3.24	5.85
70 & above	8.102	56.24	35.96	57.57	2.40	4.07
60 & above	4.655	100.00	33.56	58.62	3.46	4.36
Female						
60–64	3.297	18.07	31.90	64.43	0.69	2.98
65–69	4.723	19.83	21.12	73.05	4.56	1.26
70 & above	11.658	62.10	23.61	70.46	1.91	4.02
60 & above	6.666	100.00	24.61	69.88	2.20	3.31
Persons						
60–64	2.650	18.59	29.97	62.80	3.95	3.27
65–69	4.365	22.25	26.61	65.85	3.86	3.68
70 & above	9.644	59.17	29.57	64.25	2.15	4.04
60 & above	5.481	100.00	29.03	64.31	2.82	3.83

Table 3.15
Per Cent of Physically Immobile Men and Women in Rural and Urban Areas of Major States of the Country

	Rural		Urban	
	Male	Female	Male	Female
All India	4.4	6.8	4.7	6.7
Andhra Pradesh	4.4	7.3	3.6	5.0
Assam	5.3	6.5	7.8	7.8
Bihar	4.6	6.0	6.1	9.8
Gujarat	3.8	4.1	7.0	8.6
Haryana	5.0	3.7	1.9	5.6
Himachal Pradesh	6.7	6.8	3.1	4.5
Jammu and Kashmir	6.0	9.4	4.3	5.7
Karnataka	4.5	11.3	4.1	7.0
Kerala	6.0	8.5	4.8	6.1
Madhya Pradesh	6.5	8.8	4.5	8.7
Maharashtra	5.1	9.3	6.1	7.4
Orissa	4.9	7.1	5.4	10.0
Punjab	3.8	5.1	5.8	6.4
Rajasthan	4.0	7.2	4.4	3.7
Tamil Nadu	4.3	5.8	3.9	5.1
Uttar Pradesh	3.3	5.2	3.5	4.6
West Bengal	6.8	10.3	4.5	10.2

years, which increased to 45 in the age group of 65–69 and 55 in the age group 70+ years. The male/female differences as well as those in rural and urban areas were not significant. The pattern of chronic diseases however differed in rural and urban areas. Variations in blood pressure, heart disease, urinary problems or diabetes were apparently more common in urban areas. It is also possible that rural areas lack proper facilities for diagnosis and hence such diseases seemed less common in rural areas. Of all the old, about 45 per cent both in rural and urban areas suffered from some chronic trouble. Among these, problems of arthritic joints were the most common both in rural and urban areas. This however did not make them bedridden, as only 5 per cent or so were reported to be bedridden. But 45 per cent complaining about poor health seems in order especially when one thinks of the poverty in which people live.

While Table 3.16 does not give a statewise break-up, two points may be noted. First, the figures for Maharashtra approximated the average for India. Second, in a state like West Bengal, the incidence of blood pressure and heart disease was much higher than the national average even in rural areas. Though the details for West Bengal are not given here, one asked why this was so. Was it that heart disease and blood pressure were in fact more prevalent in rural as well as urban areas of West Bengal? Was it that West Bengal had the necessary facilities for diagnosis even in rural areas? Our guess was that the above-mentioned diseases were more common in the rural areas of West Bengal than other parts of rural India.

Table 3.17 shows the interstate variations in the proportion of chronically ill elderly in urban and rural areas for both the sexes. In most rural areas, half the states had slightly higher rates for males and in half the states females had higher rates. In other words male/female differences were negligible in rural areas. But in urban areas females had higher rates in the majority of states. Gujarat had the least percentage of chronic complainants both in rural and urban areas. Kerala, West Bengal and Assam were at the other extreme. Kerala showed the highest number of the chronically ill elderly even though generally Kerala's population enjoys better health compared to those of other states. This is possibly explained by the fact that Kerala's record in the area of nutrition is among the worst in the country as studies in this field indicated. Poverty is another reason for this high concentration of the chronically ill. But then the question arose: Why was it that Assam and West Bengal showed extremely bad conditions with regard to the chronically ill? It was difficult to answer this question without in-depth studies of these states. One may however note, as described in a later section, that Kerala, Assam and West Bengal were the states where the old people were the least gainfully active.

Old men and women in rural/urban areas were asked about ailments/injuries/poisoning, etc., and the total number of such cases was related to the total number of old persons. This was called the prevalence rate and was calculated for all age groups as seen in Table 3.18. Among these, those that were hospitalized were also noted. A person was described as hospitalized if he or she had availed of any medical services as an in-patient in any medical institution.

Table 3.16

Proportion (Per 100,000) of Persons Having Chronic Diseases and Percentage Distribution of Persons Having Chronic Disease by Type of Chronic Diseases by Sex and Age for Rural and Urban Sectors, All-India

Sex	Age	Proportion Having Chronic Disease	Types of Chronic Diseases							All
			Cough	Piles	Problem of Joints	Blood Pressure	Heart Diseases	Urinary Problems	Diabetes	
(1)	(2)	(3)	(4)	(5)	(6)	(7)	(8)	(9)	(10)	(11)

Rural

Sex	Age	(3)	(4)	(5)	(6)	(7)	(8)	(9)	(10)	(11)
Male	60–64	38.30	37.28	3.88	42.47	6.87	3.35	3.75	2.40	100.00
	65–69	44.80	34.21	3.52	47.70	5.73	3.08	3.53	2.24	100.00
	70 & above	54.86	34.89	3.90	44.14	6.36	4.35	4.68	1.68	100.00
	60 & above	45.10	35.52	3.79	44.54	6.36	3.67	4.05	2.08	100.00
Female	60–64	39.41	33.15	2.62	51.32	5.89	3.12	2.39	1.51	100.00
	65–69	44.51	33.14	2.19	49.68	6.94	4.20	2.74	1.10	100.00
	70 & above	52.62	31.85	2.51	50.51	6.76	4.29	3.07	1.01	100.00
	60 & above	44.85	32.66	2.46	50.56	6.51	3.86	2.74	1.21	100.00
Persons	60–64	38.74	35.60	3.37	46.07	6.47	3.26	3.20	2.04	100.00
	65–69	44.68	33.78	2.98	48.50	6.22	3.53	3.21	1.78	100.00
	70 & above	53.95	33.69	3.35	46.65	6.52	4.33	4.05	1.41	100.00
	60 & above	45.00	34.37	3.25	46.96	6.42	3.74	3.53	1.73	100.00

Urban

Male	60-64	36.79	24.70	4.34	34.63	18.76	7.12	4.18	6.27	100.00
	65-69	43.92	26.57	4.67	35.84	15.73	7.46	3.55	6.17	100.00
	70 & above	54.01	26.54	3.92	35.03	15.96	6.23	6.86	5.47	100.00
	60 & above	44.34	25.97	4.26	35.12	16.78	6.85	5.10	5.91	100.00
Female	60-64	39.72	23.33	2.60	44.05	18.19	5.40	1.72	4.70	100.00
	65-69	42.78	20.76	2.49	43.00	20.53	6.00	2.43	4.79	100.00
	70 & above	53.57	22.73	2.61	44.95	17.49	5.50	2.94	3.77	100.00
	60 & above	45.49	22.39	2.58	44.15	18.52	5.60	2.43	4.33	100.00
Persons	60-64	37.93	24.16	3.65	38.37	18.53	6.44	3.20	5.65	100.00
	65-69	43.45	24.25	3.80	38.70	17.65	6.88	3.10	5.62	100.00
	70 & above	53.82	24.95	3.38	39.16	16.60	5.93	5.23	4.76	100.00
	60 & above	44.82	24.52	3.58	38.79	17.48	6.34	4.02	5.27	100.00

Table 3.17
Interstate Variations in Rural/Urban Areas of Chronic Diseases Among Old Men and Women

	Rural Proportion of Chronically Ill Per 1,000		Urban Proportion of Chronically Ill Per 1,000	
	Male	*Female*	*Male*	*Female*
All India	451	448	443	455
Andhra Pradesh	560	573	525	568
Assam	639	607	643	505
Bihar	438	435	435	441
Gujarat	322	288	305	322
Haryana	367	375	360	324
Himachal Pradesh	371	359	332	344
Jammu and Kashmir	469	585	439	442
Karnataka	372	349	354	408
Kerala	691	697	707	738
Madhya Pradesh	414	393	376	426
Maharashtra	431	432	411	406
Orissa	464	517	487	554
Punjab	486	574	429	468
Rajasthan	418	364	420	382
Tamil Nadu	366	340	349	352
Uttar Pradesh	432	470	458	480
West Bengal	647	606	591	630

The data in Table 3.18 indicate that about 43 per cent of men and about 36 per cent of women in rural and urban areas had been ill or suffering and only about 10 per cent or so were hospitalized. Similarly the data for individual states (not given in the table) showed that in most of the states about 10 per cent of males and females were hospitalized in rural or urban areas. These percentages ranged between 8 to 11 per cent, with the ailing of Kerala having the highest of those hospitalized. One may conclude that hospitalization facilities did not differ much from one state to the other.

Thus, in an old population with about 45 per cent persons having chronic complaints and 5 per cent being physically immobile, it would be interesting to know how many were active in old age. It was generally believed that with agriculture as the mainstay of the population, and with poverty common in India, people tended to work as long as they could. Did they do so?

Table 3.18
Prevalence Rate (Per 1,000) and Proportion (Per 1,000) Hospitalized Among Aged Persons by Sex and Age for Rural and Urban Sectors, All-India

Sex	Age	Rural		Urban	
		Prevalence Rate	Proportion Hospitalized	Prevalence Rate	Proportion Hospitalized
(1)	(2)	(3)	(4)	(5)	(6)
Male	60–64	464	100	443	97
	65–69	324	103	342	102
	70 & above	494	102	485	100
	60 & above	427	101	423	99
Female	60–64	395	90	379	91
	65–69	278	92	298	95
	70 & above	399	97	421	94
	60 & above	357	93	366	93
Persons	60–64	436	96	416	95
	65–69	306	98	324	99
	70 & above	456	101	458	98
	60 & above	400	98	400	97

Activity Levels

What Proportion of Elderly in India was Still Active After 60 or 70 Years of Age?

The NSS 42nd Round provided data on the usual activities of men and women in rural or urban areas. Usual activity meant major time spent in gainful or non-gainful activity during the year preceding the survey. The distribution of the old men and women in rural/urban areas is presented in Table 3.19 for various age groups. The activity was classified as self-employment in agriculture (column 3, code 1); self-employment in non-agriculture (column 4 code 2); regular wage and salaried employment (column 5, code 3); and casual wage labour (column 6, code 4). Thus the total number of those gainfully employed could be obtained by adding columns 3, 4, 5 and 6. The remaining columns describe those engaged in non-gainful activity. In column 7 with code 5, one got the old who did not work but were seeking work and/ or were

Table 3.19

Percentage Distribution of Persons by Sex, Age and Usual Activity Status for Rural and Urban Sectors of Selected States, All-India

Sex (1)	Age (2)	Usual Activity Status Code									All (12)
		1 (3)	2 (4)	3 (5)	4 (6)	5 (7)	6 (8)	7 (9)	8 (10)	9 (11)	
						Rural					
Male	60–64	45.64	7.48	5.89	15.23	0.14	0.06	7.89	2.21	15.38	100.00
	65–69	40.39	6.20	2.45	12.48	0.12	0.07	7.23	2.27	28.73	100.00
	70 & above	25.02	4.38	1.53	5.34	0.09	–	6.89	3.09	53.05	100.00
	60 & above	37.96	6.21	3.62	11.48	0.12	0.05	7.44	2.49	30.63	100.00
Female	60–64	10.48	1.87	1.28	6.32	0.06	0.10	52.08	0.52	27.23	100.00
	65–69	6.11	1.63	0.50	3.00	0.09	0.07	43.36	0.77	44.47	100.00
	70 & above	2.81	0.46	0.19	0.94	–	0.08	25.51	0.89	69.12	100.00
	60 & above	6.93	1.37	0.73	3.76	0.05	0.11	41.56	0.70	44.78	100.00
Persons	60–64	31.92	5.23	4.04	11.65	0.11	0.10	25.28	1.53	20.14	100.00
	65–69	26.60	4.40	1.66	8.66	0.11	0.07	21.77	1.67	35.06	100.00
	70 & above	16.01	2.79	0.99	3.50	0.06	0.03	14.44	2.20	59.92	100.00
	60 & above	25.46	4.26	2.46	8.37	0.09	0.07	21.19	1.77	36.33	100.00

Urban

		1	2	3	4	5	6	7	8	9	Total
Male	60–64	9.89	23.75	10.57	9.04	0.14	0.12	10.66	15.28	20.55	100.00
	65–69	8.96	21.66	5.63	6.54	2.27	0.01	9.59	16.16	29.18	100.00
	70 & above	5.68	12.85	2.92	3.02	0.06	0.02	7.97	16.76	50.71	100.00
	60 & above	8.27	19.93	6.72	6.40	0.15	0.05	9.49	16.91	32.08	100.00
Female	60–64	1.52	3.78	1.39	2.07	0.03	0.62	61.28	1.64	27.68	100.00
	65–69	1.44	2.99	0.58	1.45		0.09	50.57	2.15	40.72	100.00
	70 & above	0.44	0.98	0.31	0.74	0.08	0.04	30.09	1.94	65.38	100.00
	60 & above	1.11	2.56	0.78	1.42	0.04	0.27	47.21	1.89	44.71	100.00
Persons	60–64	6.62	15.95	6.99	6.32	0.10	0.31	30.42	9.96	23.33	100.00
	65–69	5.87	14.58	3.55	4.45	0.16	0.04	26.43	10.41	34.51	100.00
	70 & above	3.41	7.71	1.79	2.03	0.07	0.03	17.57	10.33	57.07	100.00
	60 & above	5.33	12.80	4.28	4.36	0.10	0.14	24.98	10.21	37.80	100.00

Note: Usual Activity Status Code:

1 – Self-employed in agriculture.
2 – Self-employed in non-agriculture.
3 – Regular wage and salaried employee.
4 – Casual wage labour.
5 – Not working but seeking and/or available for work.
6 – Attends educational institutions.
7 – Attends to domestic duties.
8 – Rentier/pensioner
9 – Others.

available for work (called unemployed). In column 8 those attending educational institutions, mostly adult education classes, were included. Column 9 shows those attending domestic duties. In column 10 (code 8) rentiers or pensioners were included. The last category called 'others', in column 11, is dealt with in subsequent paragraphs.

Reading the Table 3.19 one finds that 46 per cent men in rural areas pursued agriculture in the age group 60–64 (see column 3). This percentage declined to 25 for ages 70 and up. A total of three-fourths of men in rural areas (columns 3 + 4 + 5 + 6) were active in the age group 60–64 and 36 per cent seemed active even after 70 years of age. In other words, it is safe to say that rural workers did not retire in sizeable numbers till 65 years of age. The number of unemployed seeking work (see column 7) was a little more than one in thousand. Clearly, the needy, required public support. Similarly in column 11 (code 9), 15 per cent men in rural areas and 21 per cent in urban areas were classified as 'others' even in the 60–64 age group. These were mostly the physically disabled or those that did not want to work for various reasons. Such numbers swelled to more than half at age 70+ among men.

Among the urban old more than half (columns 3 to 6 combined) the males were active at age 60–64. This percentage reduced to 25 by age 70+. One may also note that 15 to 17 per cent of men lived on old-age pensions in urban areas; and in rural areas this dropped to only 2 per cent or so.

As for women, one-fifth in rural areas and less than 10 per cent in urban areas were gainfully active in the age group 60–64. But they mostly attended domestic duties both in rural and urban areas. Surprisingly, the women in urban areas were more involved in domestic duties than rural women, who were more busy with agriculture or related labour.

Interstate Variations in Activity

Another area of interest was the extent to which rural/urban men and women were active in various states of the country. Did their proportions vary? If so, what were the probable reasons for such variations?

In Table 3.20 the percentages of gainfully active old urban and rural men in the 60–64 and 70+ age groups are set out for the

Table 3.20
Rural/Urban Old Men Gainfully Active in Various States

	Rural		Urban	
	60–64	70+	60–64	70+
		(age groups)		
All India	74.24	36.27	53.25	24.47
Andhra Pradesh	74.67	29.60	54.86	25.65
Assam	62.70	22.55	51.82	20.28
Bihar	71.99	33.33	57.40	23.33
Gujarat	37.96	25.77	49.73	20.57
Haryana	69.29	23.62	56.67	24.11
Himachal Pradesh	84.62	52.22	68.64	34.93
Jammu and Kashmir	80.22	47.8	63.04	30.83
Karnataka	71.22	30.95	46.79	26.32
Kerala	60.38	22.06	50.41	28.66
Madhya Pradesh	79.70	35.07	56.30	28.46
Maharashtra	72.62	30.31	48.59	21.01
Orissa	72.53	27.77	52.06	38.49
Punjab	77.77	26.33	61.87	21.39
Rajasthan	74.50	35.98	51.78	23.17
Tamil Nadu	73.24	38.34	58.21	26.74
Uttar Pradesh	75.67	52.80	60.66	27.38
West Bengal	64.81	23.32	46.46	20.43

various states. These were obtained by adding the four gainful
activities as in Table 3.19. For obvious reasons, the percentage of
those working in rural areas invariably exceeded the urban percentages in the 60–64 age group by twenty points or more. The rural/
urban differences in the percentage working after 70 years of age
was smaller though in the same direction. Himachal Pradesh was
an extreme case, with 85 per cent of rural men working in the age
group 60–64 and 52 per cent after age 70 with nobody working as
casual labour nor was in salaried service. Those who were active
probably worked at their own horticulture. Kerala, on the other
hand, showed the lowest activity, with 60 per cent of men in the
age group 60–64 and 22 per cent after age 70 in rural areas
working. Probably the old in Kerala lived on remittances of the
large majority of migrants. If one set aside these extreme cases, most
of the states looked more or less alike in the activity of the old.

Rural and urban old women were also gainfully active but to a
much smaller degree compared to men, as shown in Table 3.21. In

Table 3.21
Rural/Urban Women in Various States Gainfully Active in Age Groups 60–64 and 70+

	Age Groups			
	Rural		Urban	
	60–64	*70+*	*60–64*	*70+*
All India	19.95	4.40	8.76	2.47
Andhra Pradesh	26.53	4.73	9.07	3.17
Assam	0.48	0.41	—	0.55
Bihar	14.20	2.86	8.68	1.07
Gujarat	19.08	4.47	7.69	0.18
Haryana	5.67	—	13.24	—
Himachal Pradesh	43.68	23.79	19.11	10.30
Jammu and Kashmir	2.95	2.15	1.42	3.05
Karnataka	18.61	6.53	11.35	2.47
Kerala	12.66	1.66	2.81	2.27
Madhya Pradesh	24.92	4.12	8.62	2.27
Maharashtra	25.89	5.62	8.30	1.19
Orissa	12.73	2.62	10.61	1.42
Punjab	4.46	1.05	4.37	2.47
Rajasthan	21.23	9.25	11.74	1.62
Tamil Nadu	34.73	10.38	12.79	6.56
Uttar Pradesh	14.08	4.38	10.10	2.80
West Bengal	5.24	1.18	3.33	0.70

rural India as a whole, about 20 per cent women worked in the age group 60–64 and about 4 per cent worked even after 70 years of age. In urban India about 9 per cent worked in the age group 60–64 and about 2.5 per cent worked after 70 years of age. It was not surprising that women were much less gainfully active compared to men since they had to look after household chores. It would be interesting to see how the Indian picture of labour force participation compares with that in a developed country like the United States in 1900, 1950, 1960 and 1975 shown in Table 3.22.

Thus, female participation, though increasing, during 1900 to 1975, was much lower than that of males. The reverse was true for men during the same period. It is very likely that India, given its pace of urbanization and modernization, will show a similar trend.

According to Table 3.21, women's activity in old age appeared to be the highest in Himachal Pradesh. A possible explanation is

Table 3.22
Labour Force Participation by Age and Sex, 1900–75, USA

	Age Group	1900	1950	1960	1975
Males	55–64	93.3	86.9	86.8	75.8
	65+	68.3	45.8	33.1	21.7
Females	55–64	14.1	27.0	37.2	41.0
	65+	9.1	9.7	10.8	8.3

Source: US Bureau of the Census 1940 (in Ward, 1979: 53).

the horticulture commonly practised in Himachal Pradesh. The next active were the Tamil Nadu women. Probably the extreme poverty prevalent in Tamil Nadu explains this. The influence of poverty in keeping women active in the 60–64 age group was also seen in states like AP, Maharashtra and MP.

One may recall here the eleventh column in Table 3.19, with code number 9 constituting 'others', i.e., those that did not work, probably due to ill health. Table 3.23 presents the interstate variations in rural/urban areas for men and women in this category of 'others' for the 60+ age group. One may note that for the same sex, rural/urban differences were not very large. But both for rural and urban areas the differences between the two sexes were enormous, women constituting a much larger percentage of this category of 'others' than men. This was rather unexpected especially because women were supposed to continue with household chores even into late old age. It is possible that they were not working because of bad health which has been seen to be more common among women than men. Another explanation could be that they stopped household chores when daughters-in-law entered the home.

The only exception was Himachal Pradesh. With the least percentage in the category of 'others' or not working, this was the state with the highest percentage of the gainfully active, as evident from the data in Tables 3.19 and 3.21.

At What Age Did the People Withdraw From Work?

Old people, especially men working in agriculture were supposed to retire later than those in wage-paying or salaried jobs. The data in Table 3.24 do not show much difference in the two categories except that the difference is in the expected direction. Table 3.24 presents the percentage distribution of persons by age at retirement

Table 3.23
Men and Women of Age Group 60+ in the Category 'Others' in Rural/Urban Areas, Mostly Constituting Those Who Do not Work

	Men		Women	
	Rural	*Urban*	*Rural*	*Urban*
All India	30.63	32.99	44.78	44.71
Andhra Pradesh	33.13	33.71	50.68	47.61
Assam	38.47	33.88	50.63	45.56
Bihar	27.96	37.44	41.92	49.19
Gujarat	38.02	36.97	51.21	53.67
Haryana	42.35	34.60	58.74	53.45
Himachal Pradesh	19.40	19.38	34.97	38.86
Jammu and Kashmir	28.02	29.81	50.62	40.73
Karnataka	32.75	34.49	50.32	45.21
Kerala	36.08	31.78	43.50	44.65
Madhya Pradesh	30.95	31.93	48.05	46.75
Maharashtra	33.85	30.84	44.40	37.13
Orissa	36.78	39.68	54.38	59.43
Punjab	41.51	35.74	45.59	47.78
Rajasthan	35.82	39.68	47.11	55.29
Tamil Nadu	28.60	25.76	36.08	30.73
Uttar Pradesh	27.33	35.99	47.13	46.67
West Bengal	37.74	29.78	41.68	39.24

Table 3.24
Percentage of Persons in Rural and Urban Areas in India Who Withdrew from Gainful Activity at Given Ages in the Two Categories, Doing Own Work and Salaried Jobs

	Own Work		Jobs	
	Rural	*Urban*	*Rural*	*Urban*
−50	4.21	7.47	4.29	7.50
50–54	8.58	10.25	8.16	11.48
55–59	23.36	21.63	25.89	24.51
60 and over	64.89	60.60	61.66	56.51
Total	100	100	100	100

in two categories, namely (*i*) those engaged in gainful activity on their own and (*ii*) those engaged in wage and salaried posts.

Persons withdrew from work in rural areas to the extent of 4 per cent or so before completing 50 years whether they worked or not as salaried or wage labour. The difference in age of withdrawal in rural and urban areas was slight except that in urban areas people retired slightly earlier than in rural areas. One however expected a later withdrawal from those working on their own. But it seems that the above percentage distributions were of persons and not of men and women separately. Women in India, given their health standards, were likely to retire much earlier than men and hence the distributions as observed. Unfortunately, these figures were not available for both the sexes separately.

The reasons given by old persons for withdrawal from work were classified as: (*i*) superannuation, (*ii*) accident while at work, (*iii*) bad health, (*iv*) children capable of running the enterprise, (*v*) free from social liability, and (*vi*) winding up enterprise. The percentage distribution of persons reporting these six reasons are set out in Tables 3.25 and 3.26 for the two categories (*a*) never engaged and (*b*) ever engaged in wage and salaried jobs. These tables are for India as a whole.

One expected a large percentage reporting bad health as the reason for retirement or withdrawal from work. Of those in rural areas, 52 to 56 per cent reported bad health as the reason for withdrawal. But in urban areas, only 31 per cent reported bad health when they were working on their own while, 50 per cent urban old reported bad health when working for salary or wages. The rural/urban difference was particularly small when the persons worked on wage or salary.

When retired before 50 years, persons on their own reported old age or superannuation as the reason for retirement to a much larger extent. They did not report bad health much. Our guess was that *women working at their own agriculture or enterprise probably retired before 50 years of age (at menopause, etc.) and reported superannuation as the reason for retirement. This reporting has coloured the percentage distributions in the two tables.* It was also possible that men and women feeling less fit to work reported old age as the reason for retirement. Thus bad health and old age together accounted for 75 to 80 per cent of the retiring persons.

Table 3.25

Percentage Distribution of Persons Who Were Never Engaged in Wage or Salaried Job by Cause of Withdrawal and Age at Withdrawal from Gainful Activity for Rural and Urban Sectors, All-India

Age at Withdrawal	Cause of Withdrawal Code						All Codes	Estimated no. of Persons Engaged in Wage and Salaried Job
	1	2	3	4	5	6		
(1)	(2)	(3)	(4)	(5)	(6)	(7)	(8)	(9)
Rural								
Less than 50	53.53	2.57	29.69	7.96	3.46	2.78	100.00	240079
50–54	19.28	0.81	55.11	15.65	7.45	1.70	100.00	488976
55–59	29.55	0.94	50.65	14.64	3.49	0.73	100.00	1331795
60 & above	24.12	0.46	55.63	16.14	2.95	0.69	100.00	3549131
All	26.74	0.73	52.87	15.27	3.50	0.89	100.00	5609981
Urban								
Less than 50	60.27	2.65	18.02	6.84	3.32	8.90	100.00	65886
50–54	27.38	3.49	40.90	12.65	6.95	8.63	100.00	90404
55–59	70.05	0.40	18.76	5.53	2.46	2.81	100.00	190760
60 & above	38.23	0.78	42.09	10.85	3.93	4.13	100.00	534431
All	52.04	0.99	30.61	8.52	3.53	4.31	100.00	881481

Note: Cause of Withdrawal Code:
1 – Superannuation
1 – Accident while at work.
3 – Bad health.
4 – Children capable of running enterprise.
5 – Free of social liabilities.
6 – Winding up enterprise.

Table 3.26

Percentage Distribution of Persons Who Were Ever Engaged in Wage or Salaried Job by Cause of Retirement and Age at Retirement for Rural and Urban Sectors, All-India

Age of Retirement	Cause of Retirement Code						All Codes	Percentage of Retired Persons
	1	2	3	4	5	6		
(1)	(2)	(3)	(4)	(5)	(6)	(7)	(8)	(9)
Rural								
Less than 50	48.24	1.65	33.24	10.86	4.15	1.88	100.00	4.29
50–54	17.14	0.54	55.24	17.26	8.09	1.73	100.00	8.16
55–59	19.88	0.90	57.45	17.14	3.88	0.75	100.00	25.89
60 & above	22.47	0.45	56.30	17.14	2.96	0.68	100.00	61.66
All	22.47	0.62	55.32	16.88	3.67	0.83	100.00	100.00
Urban								
Less than 50	53.08	2.61	22.43	10.32	2.88	8.69	100.00	7.50
50–54	20.06	0.47	45.90	17.27	7.92	8.40	100.00	11.48
55–59	20.91	0.48	50.54	16.02	6.39	5.67	100.00	24.51
60 & above	19.32	0.82	54.77	15.03	4.78	5.28	100.00	56.51
All	22.35	0.83	50.26	15.17	5.39	5.99	100.00	100.00

Note: Cause of Retirement Code:

1 – Superannuation
1 – Accident while at work.
3 – Bad health.
4 – Children capable of running enterprise.
5 – Free of social liabilities.
6 – Winding up enterprise.

Financial Security

Financial Assets of the Elderly

Another area of investigation was the financial assets of the old such as company shares, government securities, Unit Trust, National Saving Certificates, etc. They were also asked about their property in the form of land and buildings. Though land as well as buildings varied enormously in value, all those having any kind of asset (from a hut or *pal* to big building) were included. The percentages are set out in Table 3.27. Since very few held such assets, the figures have been given for 100,000 as base. Thus, in India as a whole only, 581 men and 482 women in rural areas had financial assets among 100,000 men or women. This speaks for the poverty of the old. In fact it was this piece of data which revealed the enormous difference between the old in India and those in other parts of the world, especially in advanced countries. Before coming to the comparison with the rest of the world, the interstate differences are noted in Table 3.27 for both financial assets and property held.

Himachal Pradesh was found to be the richest state, with 8.5 men and 8.1 women in 1,000 in rural areas having some financial assets. This is in sharp contrast to 150 persons and 290 persons per thousand having financial assets and earnings, respectively, in the United States (Ward, 1979: 56). After Himachal Pradesh came Jammu and Kashmir, Bihar and Assam in that order. Maharashtra was worse off than the average for India. One also noted that Kerala was the poorest among the states as far as financial assets were concerned.

The property assets of the old were also noted in Table 3.27. These figures are low enough though they are better than financial assets. For rural India as a whole, 819 old men and 633 old women per 1,00,000 had property, as indicated in Table 3.27.

Thus, Table 3.27 throws enormous light on the financial conditions of old people. Generally it is believed that the older one becomes, the poorer one gets for two reasons. One is inflation and the other is the greater expenses on medication, etc. It may be true of the old anywhere but in India, even those not so old were not substantially better. This highlights the main cause of the problem in this country. In other words, the financial problems of the

Table 3.27
Proportion Per 100,000 of Persons Having Financial Assets and Property by Sex for Rural and Urban Sectors of Each State

| | Rural | | | | Urban | | | |
| | Proportion Having Financial Assets | | Proportion Having Property | | Proportion Having Financial Assets | | Proportion Having Property | |
	Male	Female	Male	Female	Male	Female	Male	Female
All India	581	482	819	633	525	371	700	481
Andhra Pradesh	375	213	727	402	363	187	614	296
Assam	708	599	859	724	760	623	856	692
Bihar	725	674	792	745	713	620	778	662
Gujarat	662	566	791	648	709	537	753	546
Haryana	284	151	841	531	397	214	812	529
Himachal Pradesh	852	813	972	899	684	573	900	773
Jammu and Kashmir	756	559	949	692	785	642	916	721
Karnataka	476	323	778	466	398	249	581	304
Kerala	259	144	772	416	354	216	724	361
Madhya Pradesh	663	552	849	691	584	444	783	593
Maharashtra	558	379	751	523	558	289	618	445
Orissa	621	587	812	728	607	618	752	766
Punjab	467	297	842	503	458	284	722	424
Rajasthan	650	544	909	799	780	658	874	814
Tamil Nadu	341	200	751	377	331	192	571	313
Uttar Pradesh	674	571	862	707	627	527	815	675
West Bengal	433	292	823	550	562	268	696	379

younger days continue into old age. Even though a large percentage worked, they were probably earning much less than their average needs including those of dependents, given that 40 per cent of the Indian population is assumed to live below the poverty line. Table 3.6 shows that about one-third of those above 60 were fully dependent on others and another 15 per cent were partially dependent (equivalent to 7.5 per cent fully dependent). Thus, about 40.5 per cent of the old could be assumed to be fully looked after by others economically. Working adults shouldered this burden in addition to the burden of children.

The conditions in rural or urban areas are equally bad. Low income in old age means poor nutrition, inadequate housing, neglect of medical services, and failure to fulfill psychological needs which were more or less non-existent in youth or were accepted as 'given'. Thus for a non-Indian the old in India presented a poor picture. But is it surprising that proper attitudes and philosophies provide the people adequate strength to face old age gracefully as revealed elsewhere in this study?

Old-Age Security

Poverty however has to be faced. It is true that money cannot buy happiness but it can certainly buy food and other amenities which the majority of the old in India lack. The social security schemes in the advanced world provide an idea as to what a rich country can do for the old. The United States began to offer social security in the mid-thirties or the depression days, and currently it is a model which is looked upon as ideal by other countries and even by the advanced ones.

As already mentioned above, the Sanjay Niradhar Anudan Yojana (SNAY) was started in Maharashtra in October 1980 which is described briefly in a later chapter. For countries like India, programmes like SNAY are the beginning of old age security. If properly developed and competently handled, SNAY will emerge as a great help to the poor old in Maharashtra and the rest of India. In fact it is one of the major sources of alleviation of poverty.

Without any old-age security, especially for the vast majority (more than 65 per cent) depending on agriculture, there is rampant poverty among the whole population and especially among the old. For those living in families the stress must be less compared to those who are helpless and who live alone. Surprisingly, when the latter were asked whether they were prepared to go to an old-age home, about 80 per cent said no even though they were given a choice about the location of these homes. For example, were they prepared to move to an old-age home if it were located in the same village (code 1, column 4), or somewhere in their own state (code 2, column 5), or somewhere outside the state? (code 3, column 6 in Table 3.28).

There were a total of 36.4 lacs of persons who were living alone in India at age 60 and over, of whom 34.23 lacs were men and 2.19 lacs women as seen in Table 3.28 (column 8). Thus, men were living alone to a much larger extent than women—a very different situation from what one comes across in the advanced world. For example, in the United States in 1975, 14.8 men and 37.3 women were living alone, as seen in Table 3.29 below.

Coming to regional variations in India, 12.4 per cent men in rural areas and 9.5 per cent men in urban areas lived alone, while only 1.4 per cent women in rural and 0.8 per cent women in urban areas lived alone (*NSS 42nd Round Report*: Statement 6, 16). Of men living alone in rural areas, only about 20 per cent were willing to move to an old-age home. Of these 20 per cent, two-thirds would move to old-age home if it were in the same village as theirs. The rest were prepared to move to a different village but in the same state. The percentage willing to move to any place outside the state was negligible. These findings were more or less true for urban areas as well. In other words the difference in rural/urban areas was not large except in the number of persons living alone which was in percentage terms smaller in urban areas. For instance one expected the number of men living alone in rural/urban India to be in the ratio 3:1 because the total population of rural/urban India was in this ratio. But it was in the ratio 294/48 or about 6:1 for men and 191/28 or 6.8:1 for women of age 60+, as seen in Table 3.28. In rural areas, 19.1 per cent of persons living alone were prepared to move to old-age homes while the percentage in urban areas was 17.6 per cent. In spite of these findings, when villagers in Maharashtra were asked to state their preferences (Chapter 5), fewer village-folk were prepared to move to such homes. This suggests that the notion of old-age homes was alien to villagers.

Table 3.28

Proportion of Persons (Per 100,000) Living Alone and Willing to Move to OAHs in Different Age Groups, and Percentage Distribution of Willing Persons in Different Age Groups by Location of OAHs for Rural and Urban Sectors (All-India)

Sex	Age	Proportion of Persons Living Alone and Willing to Move	Location of OAH Code				Estimated No. of Persons Living Alone
			1	2	3	All Codes	
(1)	(2)	(3)	(4)	(5)	(6)	(7)	(8)
Rural							
Male	60–64	20.823	63.31	32.49	4.20	100.00	1154944
	65–69	20.947	65.42	30.77	3.81	100.00	818577
	70 & above	17.493	72.76	25.94	1.30	100.00	968515
	60 & above	19.761	66.69	30.07	3.24	100.00	2942036
Female	60–64	11.272	78.08	21.92		100.00	108365
	65–69	7.215	89.96	10.06		100.00	47510
	70 & above	2.827	100.00			100.00	35518
	60 & above	8.698	81.85	18.16		100.00	191394
Persons	60–64	20.003	64.02	31.98	4.00	100.00	1263309
	65–69	20.194	65.90	30.36	3.74	100.00	866087
	70 & above	16.974	72.92	25.79	1.29	100.00	1004033
	60 & above	19.085	67.11	29.74	3.15	100.00	3133430

Urban

			1	2	3		
Male	60–64	21.944	74.09	22.32	3.59	100.00	173510
	65–69	13.982	64.23	24.57	11.21	100.00	145603
	70 & above	17.594	61.25	19.64	1.52	100.00	161694
	60 & above	18.070	71.04	21.97	6.99	100.00	480807
Female	60–64	13.780	100.00			100.00	12598
	65–69					100.00	7994
	70 & above	12.638	100.00			100.00	7311
	60 & above	9.533	100.00			100.00	27904
Persons	60–64	21.391	75.22	21.35	3.43	100.00	186109
	65–69	13.254	64.23	24.57	11.21	100.00	163597
	70 & above	17.380	72.73	19.02	8.25	100.00	169005
	60 & above	17.602	71.90	21.32	6.78	100.00	518711

Note: Location of OAH Code:
1 – Within village/town.
2 – Outside village/town but within the state.
3 – Outside the state.

Table 3.29
**Living Arrangements of Persons 65 and Above by Sex (1975)
in the United States**

	Per cent of Population	
	Men	Women
In families	79.8	56.1
Living alone	14.8	37.3
Living with unrelated individuals	1.2	1.2
In an institution	4.2	5.3
Total	100.0	100.0

Source: US Bureau of the Census (in Ward, 1979: 50).

Those living alone in various states were asked whether they were willing to go to old-age homes among the three locations described earlier. While Table 3.30 gives the statewise percentages of those willing to move to any old-age home regardless of location, the disaggregated percentages are given only for those willing to move to OAHs in their own villages or towns. They constituted a large majority among those willing to move because of their close integration with the local community. In most of the states this did hold good. But in states such as Assam, Kerala or Rajasthan they were prepared to move to any part of their state even outside their village or town. It was only in Jammu and Kashmir that the old were prepared to move mostly away even from their own state. Probably the political conditions in the state made life there un-stable. In Haryana the percentage willing to move to old-age homes was the least among the states in rural as well as urban areas.

It is understandable that the old are not prepared to move to old-age homes when they have someone to live with. This is true of the old anywhere in the world. What was surprising was the unwillingness of the old to move to such homes even when they were alone. As one can see below, this was due to the close integration of the old with the village community. For instance in rural India as a whole, 80 per cent men and more than 65 per cent women participated in social matters, with similar percentages for urban India (see Table 3.31). Participation in religious matters was only slightly higher, both among men and women. It was however surprising that household chores were also attended to by both men and women, with men participating more than women.

Table 3.30
(a) Percentage Living Alone (Not in OAHs) in
Rural/Urban Areas in Various States (b) Percentage
in (a) Prepared to Move to OAHs Anywhere
(c) Percentage of (b) Willing to Go to OAHs
Only in Their Village or Town

	a		b		c	
	Rural	Urban	Rural	Urban	Rural	Urban
All India	7.31	5.54	19.1	17.6	67.1	71.9
Andhra Pradesh	8.78	5.56	27.6	23.2	68.8	72.2
Assam	2.73	3.59	27.2	32.2	32.2	45.8
Bihar	5.91	4.99	23.5	30.8	81.6	89.9
Gujarat	7.60	8.03	10.1	13.8	66.7	70.8
Haryana	3.38	7.96	5.5	2.3	100.0	100.0
Himachal Pradesh	1.94	11.19	25.4	14.6	61.6	29.9
Jammu and Kashmir	3.33	3.96	23.0	12.8	20.0	0.0
Karnataka	5.56	4.28	15.3	18.1	42.8	88.4
Kerala	4.43	3.49	14.2	12.2	41.1	41.8
Madhya Pradesh	8.13	5.04	20.3	20.4	92.3	78.2
Maharashtra	6.66	5.22	21.2	20.3	47.8	60.6
Orissa	7.69	4.41	37.4	22.5	53.4	57.5
Punjab	4.49	6.61	22.7	29.7	59.2	57.0
Rajasthan	4.67	6.12	16.6	9.6	46.8	41.2
Tamil Nadu	11.22	5.48	20.5	19.0	54.1	71.5
Uttar Pradesh	10.73	6.79	12.7	10.8	81.2	84.6
West Bengal	5.51	3.82	35.7	13.9	68.2	68.6

Table 3.31
Extent of Participation by Old Men and Women in Social and Religious
Matters and Household Chores (Percentages)

	Participation in Social Matters		Participation in Religious Matters		Participation in Household Matters	
	Men	Women	Men	Women	Men	Women
Rural India	80.4	65.4	83.7	73.4	80.3	70.0
Urban India	80.1	66.7	85.1	75.8	77.6	67.5

Thus, about 20 per cent of men and near about 30 to 33 per cent of women did not participate in social or religious matters or in household chores probably due to immobility or bad health. It is around this social and religious participation that the life of the old revolves. It so closely integrates the old with the local society that they do not feel the need to leave their villages even when half-starved or lonely. This participation gives them psychological sustenance.

Thus, the 42nd Round of the NSSO in 1986–87 provided a rich fund of data on the old in India and the various states. Now to sum up the observations regarding the 48.2 million old people in the country: Thirty-four per cent of the old were economically independent in rural India and 29 per cent in urban India, 12 and 9 per cent of men and about 1 per cent of women lived alone in rural and urban areas respectively. Of these 18 to 19 per cent were prepared to move to old-age homes. About 45 per cent had chronic diseases. A little more than 5 per cent of the old were physically immobile. About 41 per cent in rural and 27 per cent in urban India were gainfully employed in old age. Almost all of them had no financial assets and a large majority needed public aid to alleviate their poverty.

Most of the states resembled the average for India. Maharashtra for instance rarely differed much from India. It was only a few states like Himachal Pradesh, Jammu and Kashmir, Assam, Tamil Nadu and Kerala that showed extreme observations. Himachal Pradesh, Jammu and Kashmir and Assam have mountainous areas, and Tamil Nadu along with Kerala were the poorest. These features gave them an exceptional character. But generally the pattern of living of the old was more or less similar in most states, and one wonders whether it was poverty and dependence on agriculture that were responsible for this pattern.

4

Old-Age Homes (OAHs) in Maharashtra

In the previous chapter one observed two very important aspects of aging in Maharashtra and the country as a whole. First, Maharashtra's profile of the aged was not very different from those of other states of India. This was in contrast to a few states like Himachal Pradesh, Assam, and Jammu and Kashmir which had slightly different patterns from the average due to their physical features; and Kerala and Tamil Nadu which showed some indications of extreme poverty. This was not necessarily so with Maharashtra.

The second observation was the complete integration of the old with their own community, so that more than 80 per cent of them participated in the social and religious matters of the society. This meant that less than 20 per cent or so were isolated, that too perhaps because of bad health. With this kind of integration of the old with society, among those that were alone only 20 per cent or so were prepared to move to OAHs. Of these 80 per cent were willing to move provided the OAHs were located in their own villages or towns. In other words, only less than 4 per cent were agreeable to moving to OAHs away from their native places even when living alone. This finding strongly underlined the need for opening an old-age home in each village or town. Old people occasionally suggested (as found later in this report) that they could be left in the neighbourly care of the villagers with a government grant of the old-age pensions (OAP).

OAH is a Western concept still unfamiliar in India. It means segregation of the old among their peers. There is a debate between 'age-groups isolation' and social integration in the West which has been discussed below. Since the experience of the West may be a forerunner of future trends in India, before discussing the pattern of OAHs in Maharashtra, it would be instructive to discuss the controversies such homes have generated in the West.

Debate between Age-group Isolation and Social Integration

The present apparent respect shown to old in the Orient is attributed to under-industrialization, or comparatively recent industrialization as in Japan. This school holds that the more modernized a society, the less is the respect for its old. This may partly be the case for obvious reasons. First, it is modernization (or its accompaniment namely, industrialization and urbanization) that increases longevity. Greater longevity, especially that which is attained with medication, ends in medicated survival which may not always be easy to handle. With modernization, women are less available to look after the old and the sick as they might work outside the home. Extended families become rare, which results in the need for some workable arrangement for looking after the old, especially the ailing and helpless. OAHs in the West are a partial, though not perfect, answer to this problem as seen in the subsequent discussion.

The debate generated by old-age homes is between adherents of 'community integration' and those of 'age-group segregation'. These are of course two extreme solutions. While in the West today, three generation households are regarded as incompatible with the values and structure of the modern family, there is at the same time a growing opposition to closed and isolated homes for the aged. In the present author's view, OAHs in the West have fallen into disrepute because of the medicated survival of the old beyond 80 or 85 years of age. This survival is unsatisfactory—the old of today in nursing homes are often terminally ill. The world of the sick cannot be integrated with the healthy world; the bed-ridden cannot be integrated with the active for long.

Opponents of age-group segregation cite a survey in Britain by Townsend (1962: 194) which revealed that the majority of residents deplored their transfer to an OAH and felt that it had an adverse effect on their morale. Furthermore, more than half of the residents were able to take care of themselves with either no assistance or very little; an additional fifth could live on their own if they were provided with considerable aid. The results of this survey led to a demand to abolish all old-age institutions and to transfer the care of the aged to the community where they can maintain partial independence with the help of the community and domiciliary services. As will be seen later, the story in India is not so different— the mental make-up of the aged here is similar to what one finds in the West. This is less true of the OAHs because of the different socio-economic conditions.

Advocates of semi-segregated resident settings for the old[1] hold that relationships with age peers is a major factor in the social integration of the aged. However, the semi-integrated pattern they point out works only in cases in which the aging person has been a long-term resident in a relevant, homogeneous and stable neighbourhood and as long as his network of informal relations remains localized and fairly intact. A partly segregated, age-homogeneous setting maximises opportunities for contacts with peers and protects the aged from invidious evaluation, even as it ensures that they are not cut off from outside contacts. Research of different types of semi-segregated settings has revealed extensive social participation and intensive use of the variegated facilities provided by the management.

Those recommending semi-segregated arrangements have also pointed to certain practical difficulties involved in the anti-institutional position. Given the shortage of personnel and equipment, institutionalization of a certain proportion of relatively isolated or severely disabled aged seems imperative. Furthermore, comparative analysis of different types of institutions for the aged has shown that homes that were not isolated from the community and yet allowed their residents as much privacy and independence as possible, neither cut them off from outside contacts nor produced the other adverse effects of isolated and highly bureaucratic institutionalization. It seems clear that depending on the social and economic circumstances and how advanced the aging process, people may require different interventions. Variations in temperament and value orientations also need to be taken into account.

[1] Like Shatayu Bhavan or Hingane described later in this chapter.

On the whole, intermediate patterns which combine contact and segregation, dependence and independence do away with the disadvantages of both the community integration and age-group segregation approaches.

OAHs in Maharashtra and in India

Against the above background of views on OAHs we now turn to OAHs in Maharashtra and the whole of India. Social scientists S.L. Goel and R.K. Jain (1988: Vol. 1) have described the basic structure of the OAH, which is given below. This will provide a benchmark for assessing the OAHs in Maharashtra described later. Goel and Jain suggest the broad guidelines for starting OAHs in India.

I. Objectives: Institutional care may be provided for those aged persons who have no relations to support them. Persons with families should as far as possible be encouraged to stay with them. Institutional care should therefore be provided only to the poor and destitute aged.

II. Intake: Institutions should have a definite intake policy and necessary conditions for admission into the home such as those relating to income, age, social and physical status of the person, etc. This should be laid down and followed.

Admission should be granted after an interview with the person seeking institutional care and with his immediate relations if any. There should be separate arrangements for the infirm.

III. Location and Building: (*i*) The building for an urban home for the aged should as far as possible be located on the outskirts of the city. (*ii*) The building should not cover more than 50 per cent of the total ground area. The unbuilt space should be utilized for a small garden. (*iii*) The institution should be easily approachable by local transport. (*iv*) It should have a specially constructed building with ramps instead of stairs and hand-rails for side walls. (*v*) Medical facilities if available in the nearby community should also be used by the home. (*vi*) Dormitory type of accommodation should be substituted by rooms for two to three inmates each.

(*vii*) Rooms should have proper ventilation, fresh air, light, etc. (*viii*) In cold climates porches open to the sun will be very useful. (*ix*) There should be separate rooms for reading, recreation and dining. (*x*) Easy-chairs of correct incline, beds, side tables and lockers should be provided for the inmates. (*xi*) Bathrooms should be specially constructed with handles and hand-rails, be easily accessible, and be kept clean.

IV. Food: (*i*) Food provided to the inmates should have the value of at least 2,800 calories per day. (*ii*) Four meals (two principal and two minor) a day should be served. (*iii*) The daily ration should make a light and balanced diet, with an emphasis on protective foods. (*iv*) The kitchen should be equipped with gas stoves or smokeless *chulhas*. (*v*) Fried and spicy food should be avoided.

V. Medical and Physical Care: (*i*) The home for the aged should not admit (*a*) persons needing prolonged/advanced medical care or (*b*) persons with contagious diseases. (*ii*) All inmates should be physically examined before admission, followed by periodical examinations at least once in six months. (*iii*) Persons suffering from contagious diseases and prolonged illness should be shifted to the appropriate hospital, infirmary or sanatorium. (*iv*) Adequate optic and dental care should be provided.

VI. Recreational Facilities: Recreational facilities such as a library, reading-room, a radio set, indoor games, hobbies, etc., should be provided in the home. The home for the aged could also run a day centre or a club of non-residents with like interests. This will make for regular contacts between the inmates and the other members of the community. The inmates should be encouraged to take interest in various activities, engage themselves in suitable work, and develop hobbies.

VII. General: (*i*) Necessary arrangements should be made for cremating or burying unattached persons upon their death. (*ii*) The inmates should be encouraged to participate in the planning and organization of some of the activities in the home like recreation, hobbies, preparation of menus etc. Self-government through residents' elected committees should be encouraged. (*iii*) In order to inculcate the spirit of self-help, contributions towards boarding and lodging should be invited from the inmates or their relations according to their capacity to pay.

VIII. Staff: (*i*) The success of the OAH will depend upon the type of staff running it. (*ii*) The staff should have interest in the welfare of the aged and also an understanding of their problems. (*iii*) Normally the ratio of the staff to the inmates should be 1:10 or as near to it as possible. (*iv*) Some staff members should stay on the premises of the institution. (*v*) There should be adequate nursing staff.

IX. Costs: There are not yet many homes for the aged in the country. It is therefore, not possible to find the exact percentage of expenditure on each item. However, the following broad indications will be of help.

Expenditure Heads	Percentage
Food	50–60
Clothing	5–10
Medical	5–10
Staff	15–30
Contingencies	5–10
Cremation, burials, etc.	1
Pocket money to inmates	1
Hobbies, vocational training etc.	5–10
Repairs and maintenance of building	5–10

The cost of running homes for the aged ranged from Rs. 30 to Rs. 40 per month per inmate in rural areas and Rs. 30 to 60 in urban areas (Goel and Jain, 1988).

X. Records: Previous case histories of inmates before admission, as well as proper records of progress in the home, discharge, death, etc., should be maintained in addition to a complete set of the usual establishment registers as recommended for the other residential institutions.

The above were the norms expected to be followed by OAHs. As will be seen subsequently, most of these, except those relating to housing in some cases, were adhered to by the OAHs in Maharashtra. The supervisory staff was also short of requirements in many of the OAHs.

OAHs in Maharashtra as Listed with the Welfare Department

Initially a list of OAHs in Maharashtra containing the locations of the homes and the number of inmates in them (see Table 4.1), was obtained from the Social Welfare Department of the Government of Maharashtra.

As can be seen from the Table 4.1, our survey covered 14 OAHs from the list. They were in Western Maharashtra, Vidarbha and Konkan but none from Marathwada. Budget constraints did not permit us to survey more OAHs especially those in distant places. Moreover the data regarding OAHs available from the welfare department were not complete. The OAHs listed above barring three (Hingane, Shatayu Bhavan and Widows Home) were taking grants from the government. Besides these, our survey included: (*i*) Motilal Bora (Ahmednagar, 9 inmates); (*ii*) Ambutai Mehendale (Sangli, 7 inmates); (*iii*) Navadurga (Badalapur 51 inmates); (*iv*) Chainani (Mulund, 46 inmates); and (*v*) Matrukul (Pune, 26 inmates).

Thus in the present survey of OAHs in Maharashtra, a total of 541 inmates from 19 institutions were interviewed. Out of these 363 were from institutions receiving government grants and 178 from those that did not receive such help. The questionnaire devised was meant to elicit the following information: the total number of inmates in the OAH; their housing; general structure of the building and open ground; the number of inmates per room; garden; land for agriculture and similar activities; cleanliness; common hall for recreation, prayers, etc., financing of the old-age home; government grants for upkeep of the inmates and for furnishings; donations from the public and charitable trusts; complaints and problems of those who ran the institution; and the number of deaths in their institutions.

While information on most aspects, was available, items pertaining to expenditure were sometimes inadequately dealt with since the right kind of person from the management staff was not always available to report to our investigators. Generally, however, the government grant when available was of the order of Rs. 125 per inmate. Since this proved very inadequate, the institutions were permitted to collect all kinds of donations for running the institutions, data on which will be presented in this chapter.

The OAHs have been looked at from two points of view. Part I examines the setting of the OAHs. How far was the setting capable

Table 4.1
Location of OAH, Number of Inmates Reported by Social Welfare Department, and Number Found in the Survey

District and Region	Name of the Institution	No. of Inmates Reported	Number Found in the Survey
Konkan			
Thane	Shantiprakah Vriddhashram, Ulhasnagar	75	75
Western Maharashtra			
Bombay	Shraddhananda, Matunga	50	47
Ahmednagar	Phirodia OAH	95	83
Pune	1. David Sassoon Infirm Ashram called Niwara	70	70
	2. Widows' Home, Solapur Road†		14
	3. Home for Blind Women, Dhayari†	25	24
	4. Hingane		62
	5. Shatayu Bhavan† Pune Vidyarthi Griha		26
	6. Ishaprem Niketan, Padamji park, Pune	35	No survey
Sangli	Vriddhasevashram, Kupwad	25	20
Solapur	W.B.N. Ba Akashashram, Pandharpur	15	No survey
Vidarbha Region			
Amravati	1. Madhuban Vriddhashram	35	13
	2. Gadge Maharaj, Valgaon	30	20
	3. Gurukunja Ashram, Mozari	30	20
	4. Takshashila	15	No Survey
Nagpur	1. Untakhana*	100	20
	2. Panchavati	50	46
	3. Shrikrishnashram	20	No survey
Akola	Sanjay Gandhi Vriddhashram, Kasarkhed	20	No survey
Buldhana	Gadge Maharaj Vriddhashram, Dahigaon	10	No survey
Parabhani	Jagruti Mahila Vriddhashram, Kalampuri	10	No survey
Marathvada			
Nanded	Indira Gandhi Mahilashram run by Babasaheb Ambedkar Educational Institution, Khurda Loni	10	No survey

* This Christian organization was very unwilling to permit us to interview its inmates so we interviewed only 20 inmates.

† These were not getting grants from government.

of satisfying the demands of the inmates? Or how far did it conform to the guidelines for OAHs described earlier?

The perspective of the inmates themselves is dealt with in Part II. For instance, what kind of people were they? Why were they driven to come to OAHs? What were their problems in remaining with their own families? Were they happy in the OAHs?

Part I: The Setting of the OAHs

Location

Certainly the OAH should be located in a pleasant, quiet atmosphere. It should neither be too far away from a railway station or state transport bus stop, nor too close since heavy traffic and hubbub of the stations can put an unbearable strain on the old and infirm. Marketing facilities had to be in the vicinity. The road from the OAH to the hospital must be in good shape so that old patients can be taken in an ambulance without much trouble. From this point of view 13 out of 19 OAHs (Shraddhananda in Vasai, Vriddhasevashram in Kupwad [Sangli], Hingane, Widows' Home, Matrukul, Shatayu Bhavan, Niwara, Phirodia and Motilal Bora in Ahmednagar, Chainani in Mulund, Untkhana and Panchavati in Nagpur, and Gurukunj Ashram in Mozari, Amaravati) were suitably located. Navadurgashram at Badlapur was at the foot of some hills and about 5 kilometers from the railway station but the road was very bad. Madhuban was about 10 kilometers from the railway station in an isolated place and the institution had no vehicle of its own. Gadgebaba Valgaon was 15 kilometers from the railway station and 4 kilometers from Valgaon village making communication difficult. Dhayari OAH for the blind was 15 miles from Pune but at least bus transport was available. Both Shantiprakash Vriddhashram in Ulhasnagar and Mehendale Ashram in Sangli were in the midst of busy towns and market areas.

Availability of Open Ground

OAHs should have some open ground so that the old could move about freely and safely for exercise, relaxation or peace of mind. In vacant land it is possible to grow fruits, vegetables or flowers if

water is available in plenty and some help from a healthy, know-
ledgeable person is forthcoming. This creates a pleasant atmosphere
around the OAH, and the old can occupy themselves with the
upkeep of the garden in addition to enjoying the fruits of their
labour. Kitchen-gardening can also generate some income.[2] For
this outside help from willing young and old can be taken.

In Mozari, Gurukunj Ashram, the premises of which were kept
very clean, stood on 10 acres of land. There were many trees and a
garden too. Phirodia and Motilal Bora, two sister institutions,
were spread over 5 acres of land. A few fruit and flowering trees
livened the homes. The managers of the institution planned to
involve the students in growing fruit and other trees in the premises.
Around Shatayu Bhavan about 150 coconut and other trees adorned
the open space. In Niwara, the home named after David Sassoon,
standing on 5 acres, vegetables grown with the help of the aged
made the place at least partly green. Dhayari, a blind women's
home had a few flowering trees and a small but neat garden. The
inmates, could not enjoy the sight but the premises certainly
looked lovely to others. The blind enjoyed using the swings kept in
the garden. In Vasai there was a little open space with a few
flowering trees, the blossoms of which were strung by the old to
make garlands. Others like Untakhana and Panchavati in Nagpur,
Madhuban in Amravati, Gadgebaba in Valgaon, and Vriddhasevashram in Kupwad, Sangli, had limited open space and water.
The land was not being used at the time of the survey but the plan
was to create additional housing on the premises since the institutions were rapidly expanding.

Badlapur Navadurga Ashram was surrounded by adequate open
land, but water shortage was the limiting factor. Efforts were
underway to procure more water so that gardening could be explored.
Mehendale OAH had a few trees. Chainani had no land, only four
cement benches outside. Matrukul being at the foot of a hill
temple had more than 100 well-constructed steps, and women in
the OAH could go up these steps according to their capacities. In
the Ulhasnagar OAH there was no open space at all. The Widows
Home had space but it was unkempt and the neglected appearance
of the premises made a striking contrast to the cleanliness inside

---

[2] In Niwara OAH, they sold bananas worth Rs. 200 a day for three years
continuously.

the home. Perhaps only 14 inmates, most of whom were disabled, did not encourage the administrators of the home to tidy the premises.

The Lodging Arrangements of the Homes

In their own homes, the old lived among young people who were mobile and busy. Even if infirm, the elderly somehow pulled along with the rest. But in an OAH most of the inmates were frail and had limited mobility. Besides, they might be slovenly and untidy, obstinate and bad-tempered, too talkative or withdrawn—all of them had to be kept satisfied and catered to in an OAH.

Most of the residents either lived free or paid a nominal fee. Thus, 263 inmates paid nothing, 100 whatever little they could afford, and 178 according to the rules of the particular OAH. Where most of the elderly lived free, the OAHs collected grants from the government. Those who could afford to pay Rs. 450 to 700 or so per month lived in homes that did not accept government grants. There was a marked difference between the lodging arrangements of the two kinds of homes. Another difference was in the level of neatness between inmates. Those that were immobile depended on the administration and the staff. The living arrangements of the inmates also depended on the availability of housing and the regulations of the OAH.

A one-person-per-room arrangement was available in Chainani Vriddhashram, Hingane and Navadurga. In Chainani a room with a toilet was available for Rs. 700, which also included food. There were 11 such rooms there. In Hingane and Navadurga a single room for the rest of the inmate's remaining life was available for Rs. 20,000 and 21,500, respectively, as a gift. While Hingane had 48 such rooms, Navadurga had 4, with 4 more under construction. They had space to construct additional ones too. A room with a toilet and a small counter for a cooking-stove was available for a couple in Shatayu Bhavan, Motilal Bora and Hingane. This arrangement was available in Shatayu Bhavan for Rs. 10,000 as gift and Rs. 30,000 as deposit, and in Motilal Bora for Rs. 2,000 as a gift and Rs. 300 per annum. This was quite reasonable. A double room in Hingane fetched Rs. 30,000 as a gift. In Chainani for a double room, including food, each one had to pay Rs. 500. In Mehendale there were three single and double rooms each. The payment for both types of rooms was the same. There was no attached toilet with either.

The pattern of housing in most of the OAHs was as follows. Homes not accepting government grants housed 3 to 5 inmates in a sizeable room (area about 125 to 150 sq ft) since they charged for housing. Those that accepted grants held 6 to 15 residential cots in dormitories (area about 150 to 500 sq ft). With such arrangements, care had to be taken that no one was disturbed. For those who preferred a dormitory arrangement, there were 5 to 10 people to take care of them if necessary.

In Madhuban, Amravati, all 29 mobile and immobile inmates were housed in one big hall. In Ahmednagar 35 to 50 mobile women were similarly kept. As a permanent arrangement, this was no doubt unsatisfactory. In most of the other OAHs the housing seemed all right. In Phirodia OAH, there were three latrines and two bathrooms each for men and women. While the administration considered these many latrines and bathrooms to be sufficient for 50 men and women each, the 38 men and 48 women living there found them to be inadequate.

Furnishing for the Individual Inmates

All the inmates from all the OAHs were provided with cots, adequate bedding, individual clothing, and a small bag or chest for keeping their things. Those OAHs that accepted government grants supplied two sets of clothes and a couple of plates and containers for food and snacks to the inmates. Each one was required to clean and take care of one's own set of things. OAHs which did not receive state funds did not provide clothes or bedding; utensils for food and snacks were managed and cleaned by the staff of the homes. As for laundry, inmates had to make their own arrangements or pay for it. In Mulund and Ulhasnagar a washerman visited regularly. In Mehendale and Navadurga the girls from the neighbouring orphanage were available for doing the laundry on payment. Motilal Bora inmates could get their clothes washed by the able-bodied residents of Phirodia OAH on payment. Generally, hot water was available daily for bathing for all the inmates. Phirodia home was an exception, with hot water being provided only twice a week. Hence many inmates did not bathe daily.

Dining-Hall

In most OAHs there was a kitchen, storeroom and administration wing. Besides, there was the dining-hall, prayer rooms and recreation rooms. In some cases, one room was used for all these purposes.

In Hingane there was no common kitchen, dining-room or storeroom because the inmates made either their own cooking arrangements or got their food from the girls' school boarding-house which was in the premises. In some homes the inmates sat on their cots with their plates and containers and the staff of the home served them the food or snacks. This kind of arrangement was seen in the Widows' Home or the Mehendale home. In others there was a specific area where food or snacks were served and the inmates helped themselves with the assitance of the staff. In Shanti-prakash the inmates brought their eatables from such a place and ate them sitting on their own cots. Shraddhananda, Motilal Bora, Phirodia, Navadurga, Chainani, Niwara, Matrukul, Shatayu Bhavan and the Blind Women's Home all had separate dining-halls.

When inmates were temporarily ill their neighbours helped out by bringing food or washing their utensils; if permanently bedridden, the staff of the OAH served them and also washed their utensils.

Prayer Room or Meditation Hall

Many OAHs made separate arrangements for prayer. Generally the old were expected to visit these halls at specific times where they prayed or sang bhajans for an hour or so everyday. They could practise meditation too if they chose. In the same hall, all kinds of recitals *pravachan* (religious discourse), *keertan* (devotional songs), or vocal music programmes by outsiders were arranged for the recreation of the old. Shraddhananda, Phirodia, Shanti-prakash, Chainani, Home for Blind Women, Widows' Home and Gurukunj at Mozari had separate prayer halls. In Shraddhananda, Shantiprakash and Chainani they had their prayer halls on the first of their three-storey buildings. In Phirodia there was a shed which was used both for dinning and prayer. Widows' Home designated time for prayer twice a day.

In all the OAHs inmates were free to pray on their own, and there was no pressure at all on anybody to participate either in the collective prayer sessions or any other programme. In Vasai, for instance, among the majority who were Hindus, there was one Gond tribal Christian woman who said her own prayers in the same hall along with the others. In the Widows' Home among all the Christian women, there was one Bengali Hindu woman who said her own prayers. In the Phirodia home there was one Muslim who said his prayers to his own satisfaction. Though there were fixed times, the inmates usually participated according to their own will and enjoyed such get-togethers. These programmes which took them a short distance away from their rooms, seemed quite popular—here they could forget their aches and pains or everyday cares in the midst of the crowd. In David Sassoon's Niwara and the home in Kupwad Sangli, there seemed to be no regular time for prayer. Homes which did not accept grants from the government did not generally have prayer halls, e.g., Motilal Bora, Mehendale, Navadurga, Shatayu, Matrukul and Hingane. Chainani was the only exception to this rule. This was probably because coming from economically better backgrounds, the inmates from these homes chose to engage themselves independently—in reading or playing cards, watching TV or listening to the radio, taking a walk or busying themselves in their own private Yogasana or meditation. They probably preferred doing these activities in smaller groups or alone.

Daily Routine

In most of the OAHs inmates got tea twice a day, breakfast at about 9 AM, and two meals a day. In Phirodia and Motilal Bora, they got a cup of milk with breakfast. In Shantiprakash, besides tea, main meals and breakfast, all inmates got a cup of milk at night. In Nagpur, inmates got one piece of fruit everyday after lunch. Timings for tea, breakfast and meals were more or less fixed in all the OAHs, Occasionally breakfast and meals were kept aside for persons if they had informed earlier. In Matrukul no breakfast was served. This was the only exception.

Each inmate was required to make his or her own bed and keep the floor under it clean. Generally, keeping the room or dormitory clean was the collective responsibility of the inmates. Thus they busied themselves in keeping their things and clothes clean, observing timings for meals and breakfast, participating in common prayers, and spending time with those that got along with them temperamentally.

In most of the OAHs there was an unstated rule that the inmates helped in the routine work of the OAH according to their capacity or ability. In the OAHs where the inmates paid a monthly fee, this routine work mostly meant only cleaning the vegetables. In those OAHs which accepted government grants, the healthy inmates were required to help in cooking, serving food, washing utensils and bathrooms, keeping the premises clean, shopping, paying bills, getting men for repairs of the OAH, etc. This kind of work had to be done in Niwara, Phirodia, Shantiprakash, Gadgebaba, Gurukunj, Madhuban and Panchavati. In Shraddhananda, the Blind Women's Home and Kupwad Sangli, on the contrary, the inmates had little responsibility.

Since all the inmates got food, some rest and leisure time, medication if necessary, company of their peers, and a safe environment in the OAHs, the inmates seemed happy to help out. Of course some staff was necessary to assist the old inmates and coordinate and allot their work in turns. In addition, the individual inmates were free to offer some worship, read religious texts, or recite from the scriptures. Those that were weak and infirm had limited energies, so that paying attention to cleanliness and taking rest were enough to keep them occupied. Not surprisingly, when the inmates of OAHs accepting government grants were asked for their suggestions for improving the homes, hardly any were forthcoming, as will be found later in this study.

Library Facilities

Most of the OAHs got a couple of newspapers and the menfolk seemed interested in reading them. There seemed limited interest among women on account of their illiteracy and the fact that most of them had spent time in casual labour or domestic work during their lives. Hence in the OAHs which received government grants, women rarely read newspapers. Some OAHs kept old magazines and books. Thoughtful citizens regularly provided their magazines to such OAHs, and the literate inmates certainly enjoyed reading them. Niwara, Shraddhananda, Gurukunj, Madhuban, Navadurga, Mehendale, Shatayu, Matrukul, Hingane and the Blind Women's Home all had some kind of a library. In the last-mentioned home there were some books in Braille, but the women could not read them because in their younger days they had not learnt to use Braille. However, some citizens of Pune used to regularly go to this home to read to the blind, and most women seemed to enjoy listening to the reading. In Mehendale, staff members read to the old. This OAH had a sister institution, an orphanage, with a reasonably good library, which could be used by its inmates. Hingane used the library of the big school on the premises. Some citizens gave away their unwanted books on philosophy or school texts to the OAHs. But the readers complained that such books were of no use—they only collected dust and should not be accepted by the libraries.

Recreation

Inmates enjoyed people coming to the OAH to read to them regularly. They used to eagerly wait for the reader in Shraddhananda as well as in the Blind Women's Home in Dhayari. A couple from Vasai used to visit Shraddhananda and read religious texts which most inmates found interesting.

In every society there are a few people who are prepared to devote some of their leisure time in helping others. OAHs should enlist the services of such people, but they should be regular, punctual, and have empathy for the inmates.

In Badalapur's Navadurgashram, a gentleman from Dadar used to visit the home every Sunday from 6 AM to 4 PM. For those who were not very mobile he would bring medicines, non-perishable eatables, things for their everyday needs. He also obtained tickets for inmates wanting to travel, saw them off at the railway or bus station, tried to get specific books from the library or returned them, carried messages, wrote letters and so on. This gentleman came from a lower middle-class household with limited means and a middle level education. However, he earnestly felt that this kind of work helped him to serve God and thus gave him satisfaction. If more such voluntary workers were to be available to the OAHs, much happiness can be given to the old and suffering.

Another type of recreation in the OAHs, apart from reading, was the common singing of bhajans or chanting of religious or other texts. Often there would be somebody among the inmates who could lead such programmes knowledgeably. As long as they could participate and get engrossed, the inmates did not bother about their musical abilities because in such group activities they could forget their everyday worries and rise above their envies and petty quarrels. This elevation of the mental and spiritual atmosphere of the OAHs was experienced by most homes which had routine prayers, singing of bhajans or recitations.

Television and radio sets were generally available in the OAHs. Along with books, magazines and newspapers, the recreation facilities were more or less adequate. Rarely were the old interested in playing games such as cards, carrom, chess, etc. Nor did they mention such games for recreation when asked to make suggestions for improving the OAH facilities. Providing these games was certainly not costly, but may be the inmates had never played them in their younger days.

Medical Facilities

In any institution where there is a group of people staying together, some basic medicines and medical equipment have to be stored. This is particularly so in an OAH because the large majority of inmates periodically need some sort of basic medical aid. Simple aches and pains may turn out to be indications of chronic disease and acquire serious proportions. If controlled early, the old can live a comfortable life naturally. Moreover, the administration would want the old to be mobile and comfortable rather than immobile and bedridden. In many cases medical experts were prepared to visit the OAHs periodically to treat and advise the inmates. OAHs which accepted government grants often kept a medicine chest for the use of the inmates. Two out of 11 institutions accepting grants, Panchavati from Nagpur and Gadgebaba from Valgaon, had no such medicine chests. Three grant-receiving homes Niwara, Phirodia and Kupwad, transferred the sick to the government hospitals. Shraddhananda, Vasai, had given a grant of Rs. 200,000 to a local hospital for reserving four beds for its inmates. Shantiprakash and Gurukunj in Mozari each had a hospital run by voluntary organizations in the town. Thus all these three institutions were well-equipped to provide medical aid.

In homes which did not accept grants and where inmates paid a monthly fee, the inmates were expected to make their own arrangements for medical help. The three exceptions to this were Navadurga,

Chainani and the Widows' Home in Pune. Here the doctors visited the homes on specific days and prescribed the necessary medicines. Generally most of the OAHs kept a stock of the medicines that were usually required; if other medicines were needed, the inmates had to make their own arrangements. In Chainani the inmates had to pay the paltry sum of Rs. 2 to the establishment for consultation from the doctors who visited the home. One thing deserves specific mention. Those that were mentally disturbed, were given the prescribed medicines only by the staff, who made sure that the medicines were taken. This was particularly so in Navadurga and Niwara. In the latter some medical specialist or the other visited the home everyday, and one day was reserved for the mentally handicapped. In all the OAHs there was always somebody requiring professional psychiatric help. In Niwara the establishment ran a physiotherapy centre for three hours every morning which could be used by the inmates as well as outsiders. Outsiders had to pay which helped the centre's finances.

Inmates suffering from serious fever or from fractured bones had to be helped. Similarly those suffering from asthma or heart trouble needed some help. Home for Blind Women, Shraddhananda and Navadurga maintained a couple of needy, healthy persons for this purpose. They assisted the immobile or weary. In Phirodia the healthy inmates themselves helped others and made a little money. One way of dealing with the seriously ill of course was to shift them to a hospital in an ambulance. But this was not always possible, nor were the hospitals prepared to keep the patients beyond a stipulated period. Moreover such an arrangement is expensive; it is not always possible for the inmates to pay at the eleventh hour. Hence at the time of admission, the inmates were often expected to deposit some lump sum with the homes, if possible, which could be used in times of emergency. Sometimes any amount remaining with the home was paid back to the heirs of the deceased. This was seen to be the case in Motilal Bora and Navadurga. Niwara home maintained some staff who could help in nursing the sick. Matrukul, Shatayu, Hingane, Chainani and other homes accepting regular payments warned the inmates, at the time of entry that they would not be allowed to stay in the homes if seriously ill or disabled. In fact, the relatives of the old were expected to take them away in such circumstances. In other words, the establishment was not prepared to take on any responsibility for them when sick or disabled. It was only in the Widows' Home that the inmates were looked after well even when ill.

Whenever there are old persons, some are bound to be bedridden. If the homes had some able-bodied staff, they had to do two totally different kinds of chores. Healthy persons were needed to clean the floors, wash clothes, work in kitchen or garden, to take some inmate out. In India, given our standards, workers are available for these kind of tasks. A far more difficult chore is looking after the bedridden and seriously ill. In fact some nursing staff is needed which the OAHs could not afford.

Those OAHs that accepted payment from the inmates did not assume responsibility for them when they were bedridden. This seemed to us their weakest point. What good were OAHs if they did not take care of the sick? OAHs which declined responsibility for the bedridden therefore attained the status of an inexpensive hotel where the paying guests met only members of their age group. But if they were to become disabled, would they be readily accepted by their relatives when the OAH did not accept them? Paid nursing homes could be one alternative; but these are mostly not available. India has two very different kinds of nursing facilities: ill-equipped, understaffed, free government hospitals for the vast majority and extremely expensive hospitals for a select few who can afford them. Nursing of the terminally ill is going to be a serious problem in future and the paid homes available today, with their steep costs, offer no solution. From this point of view, even the grant-receiving OAHs seemed to be more aware of the problem and had an inexpensive solution for it. The inmates were taken care of at the level they could afford or the OAHs could afford and these two levels generally agreed except in the case of the terminally ill, who are difficult to treat.[3] Though the care of the old was at a low level, the inmates did not complain, having been used to it most of their lives.

[3] Here, as an example, a case of rough handling of a bedridden patient may be mentioned. This person had been kept in a government hospital which did not keep terminally ill patients. So the OAH was asked to take away the patient after his due treatment. But the OAH delayed action for a day, upon which the hospital brought the sick person in an ambulance and left him at the door of the OAH.

It is only a matter of time before the problem of the terminally ill assumes serious proportions in India. Since the medical help available presently is very limited and expensive, the problem has acquired some urgency only in the small middle class.[4] The lower longevity among the poor obviously means that relatively few suffer from terminal illnesses. With a wider dispersion of medical services, a larger proportion of the country's population will have to contend with this problem. Today even an affluent country such as United States finds it difficult to run nursing homes for the terminally ill. In Britain nursing facilities used to be provided in people's homes which partly took care of the problem. In cities like Pune some voluntary agencies provide a nursing help to the old in their own households if paid adequately, but most cannot afford it. In any case this does not adequately address the question of the terminally ill because the problem of supervision of the paid worker will remain unsolved especially when the old are living alone and without family. How can even the paid worker offer sympathetic service to the old and disabled?[5] Nursing homes even in the United States have fallen into disrepute partly because the workers lacked the necessary sympathetic attitude to the terminally ill, and the supervision fell short of what was required.

In India a sympathetic attitude from the nursing staff was lacking among the Hindus unlike in the Christian homes. In addition to the care of the bedridden, attention to the cleanliness of the toilets and bathrooms was also inadequate in most of the non-Christian OAHs. In the Widows' Home, Pune, the nursing of the disabled seemed perfect. Even though the inmates here did not come from well-to-do families, they were well looked after. Our guess was that these church-run homes were relatively much better funded than the other OAHs, but it was difficult to get reliable data on

[4] Niwara OAH had opened a convalescent home where the daily charge was Rs. 25 without food. This was perhaps the lowest charge for the terminally ill both among the OAHs as well as outside.

[5] Mrs. D in Pune, an old lady aged 83, did not join her only son in Assam, 1,500 miles away. So the son maintained a maid to look after his mother with medical help from a doctor. Being bed-ridden she had had bed sores, and a weekly visit from the doctor was inadequate. The maid did not take proper care of the mother so that when she died people found that ants had bitten the old lady. The maid exclaimed loudly after the mother's death saying how she herself had done so much for the lady and still she died. Actually, the maid had neglected the lady and this was discussed by the neighbours but no one helped out.

this point from them. In fact Untakhana, a Christian OAH, did not allow us to freely interview its inmates.

Help from the Supplementary Institutions

The presence of other institutions on the premises or in the neighbourhood of an OAH helped enrich its atmosphere. The old did not remain completely segregated and the home was enlivened with activity. Instances of such supplementary institutions are described below.

1. The Mehendale Old-Age Home had a sister institution for orphaned girls on its premises. The library for these girls was shared by the old. Besides, the grown-up girls helped the elderly in washing clothes and sweeping the floors, and accompanied them to the nearby market, garden or dispensary. They also helped out with a little marketing for the old. On their part, these orphaned girls could get a few words of sympathy or appreciation from their elderly neighbours.

2. In Navadurgashram in Badalapur, the inmates shared the OAH with a few grown-up, mentally handicapped women. Though healthy, energetic and capable, these women were unwanted by their households. Moreover, at home they were open to the threat of abuse by anti-social elements. In an institution they could be safe and get sympathetic treatment. They worked for the old, fetched hot water for their baths, brought breakfast to the ill, and carried messages.[6] The mature among the old would treat them sympathetically. The supervisory staff could see that the relationship was harmonious.

3. In Hingane Old-Age Home, there were two or three other buildings on the premises, comprising a school and hostels for a few hundred girls. Their library was used by the inmates of the OAH. Besides, some of the old could help the girl students with their studies. Moreover, a number of school socials were held on the premises which livened the atmosphere for the old. In the

---

[6] In Panchavati a physically handicapped boy used a rickshaw to transport the immobile old to the temple on the premises.

midst of young girls jumping around happily with no worries or responsibilities, the old certainly forgot their aches and pains and the disappointments of life.

4. Near Matrukul at the Foot of the Parvati Hills, there was a home for helpless women and also a hostel for earning women. All these women ate as well as lived together. The old were exposed to a wider world; they mingled with people whose experiences or backgrounds were different from what they had known. The helpless women had troubles of a different kind. Observing these, the old forgot their own ills, enjoyed exchanging ideas, or offered a few words of sympathy. This certainly gave them more confidence to face their own ills.

5. The Shraddhananda Home of Vasai. This also housed orphans of 3 to 5 years of age and ran a creche too. Some of the old took on the role of grandmothers and experienced the love of grandchildren.

6. Attached to Mozari was 10 Acres of Land. A school, library, temple, hospital and printing press were all located on it. The old enjoyed the proximity of the temple and library and availed of the hospital facilities. In the premises there was the *samadhi* (tomb) of a well-known saint whose teachings had elevated the atmosphere and minds of the neighbours. His life story gave the old courage to face their sufferings. In fact all the institutions on the premises were named after this saint who had donated all his earnings to them.

7. In Gadgebaba Home for the Old in Valgaon, many facilities were lacking. However, those who lived here believed that they were serving Gadgebaba or God and this faith helped them to bear their suffering.

8. Niwara had a Convalescents' Home and a Physiotherapy Centre, while these facilities could be used by the inmates, they were available to outsiders for a fee, so as to make the OAH economically productive. The presence of outsiders on the premises was no doubt welcome. The convalescent home had 32 beds, of which 24 were meant for outsiders and 8 for the inmates. The daily charge for staying there was Rs. 25, including help at the *dai* (minimally qualified nurse) level. It was a deliberate policy of this home not to provide the convalescents with food. Niwara strongly believed in families taking care of their invalid old—by supplying food the relatives kept alive their bonds with the elderly.

Our findings on the 19 old-age homes surveyed by us may be summed up as follows. The two kinds of homes, those that accepted payments from the inmates and those that received government grants differed in various ways. Surprisingly, some of those which charged their inmates did not provide better service than those which catered for the poor, especially on the question of accepting the responsibility for the seriously or terminally ill. Their refusal to do so degraded their status to an inexpensive hotel for old peers. Relatively speaking, the ones run for the poor with government grants showed more awareness of the main problem of the old—the possibility of their becoming completely immobile. In fact when mobile, the old did not need much help except for some money. But when bedridden, a lot more beside money was needed, and that was reasonably available in the poor homes. In India what is needed for the majority are such homes. Of those accepting payment, Navadurga was the only home which looked after the old till the very end.

In short, with the immobile or terminally ill it is important to understand the value of what can be called 'family'—an institution best placed to give support of the non-monetary kind. There remain many problems, solutions for which elude even the rich. Can poor India find the answers? It can, provided old family traditions are maintained and modernization does not erode human values and a sympathetic attitude, which is integral to any meaningful solution.

Deaths

Given the disinclination of the privately run homes to accept responsibility for the seriously or terminally ill, deaths mostly occurred in the OAHs getting government grants. In our survey of OAHs, the home for widows and Navadurga, though not accepting grants, had deaths and bedridden patients too. The deaths during the previous year in each of the government-funded homes which did not turn away seriously or terminally ill patients and their total number of inmates are shown in the Table 4.2 below.

Table 4.2
**Institutions, Number of Inmates, and Total Number of Deaths in Them
in the Previous Year (1990–91)**

Institution	Number of Inmates	No. of Deaths in the Previous Year
Niwara	70	16
Phirodia	83	10
Shraddhananda, Matunga	47	7
Kupvad, Sangli	20	3
Shantiprakash	75	7
Gadgebaba	28	1
Madhuban	29	4
Home for Blind Women	24	3
Gurukunj, Mozari	20	2
Total	396	53

Thus, the death rate in government-aided OAHs (where the inmates who became terminally ill were not asked to leave) was approximately 125 (i.e. 53 × 1000/396 + 26.5). The expected death rate above age 60 for the general populace was 52.6* per thousand for India during 1988–89[7] which was much lower than that found in poor OAHs. Among the OAHs which did not receive government grants, Navadurga and the Widows' Home, which looked after the old till the end had 9 deaths with 44 inmates. Other homes, with inmates paying some fixed sums but being asked to leave if seriously ill, had 10 deaths and 175 inmates. Thus, the death rate per thousand among them was approximately 55, which was much lower than that in the poor OAHs (125) for two reasons. First, they certainly came from a better off class; second, they had to leave the OAH if they became seriously ill.

* 7	Death Rates for Age 60+ Per 1000 for Rural/Urban India by Sex		
	Men	Women	Total
Rural	56.7	49.0	52.8
Urban	57.2	48.2	51.4
Combined	56.8	48.3	52.6

Source: Sample Registration Scheme (1989).

With OAHs having recently become aware of the expenses that are incurred after an inmate dies, some of those which charge a fee have started taking deposits of the order of Rs. 2,000 to 3,000 to take care of such contingencies.

Payment Given to the OAHs by the Inmates

Of the 541 inmates surveyed, 178, i.e., one-third, lived in institutions that did not accept grants from the government but charged the inmates some reasonable sum. The remaining 373 (i.e., 69 per cent) resided in homes that received government funds, which amounted to Rs. 125 per person. This being obviously inadequate, the institutions were permitted to collect donations from the public. Of the inmates of grant-receiving homes, 273 persons (i.e., 73 per cent) lived free and the rest paid some small monthly amount (not necessarily fixed) either from their pensions or savings. The methods of payment to the institutions by the inmates or the public are shown in Table 4.3.

To conclude, one got the impression that notwithstanding the few drawbacks of old-age homes, the elderly, including the poor, in these institutions were happily placed. They worked, took exercise or went for walks to the extent of not exhausting themselves; when tired they lay on their beds. When they felt the need to relax they talked with their peers or watched television. They did not feel embarrassed because they could not work nor move as quickly as the others in their own households. They could eat in peace without feeling that they had not earned enough to enjoy their meal, which they might have felt in their own homes. Nobody taunted them for lying down. Moreover, the old did not have to worry about their food—this was given at stipulated times. Earlier, before coming to the old-age home, perhaps they used to feel lonely and unsafe. May be their meals were not given to them kindly. Probably they were treated unsympathetically by younger people. But no more of that in the OAH. Some told woeful stories about their past. Now that they were accepted along with their handicaps, they could manage in spite of a few inconveniences with a peaceful mind.

It is a common perception that nobody goes happily to an old-age home. That the elderly who have been 'deserted' find refuge in such institutions, somehow dragging out their lives in them. That

Table 4.3
Method of Payment to OAHs by Inmates

Institution	Amount (Rs.) Deposited	Gift	Monthly Payment	Remarks
1. Niwara (Pune)	Nil	Nil	Nil	See footnote 1
2. Phirodia (Ahmednagar)	Nil	See footnote 2	Proportion from pension*	
3. Motilal Bora	2000	Rs. 300 per year	Rs. 350	
4. Shraddhananda (Vasai)	Nil	Savings, gold, etc.	Proportion from pension*	
5. Kupvad (Sangli)	Nil	Nil	Rs. 100 if possible	
6. Shantiprakash (Ulhasnagar)	Nil	footnote 2	–	Institution paid Rs. 20 a month as pocket money to the inmates
7. Gadgebaba	Nil	Nil	Nil	
8. Vridha Apangasewa (Utakhana)			Nil	
9. Panchavati (Nagpur)	a) Earlier nil b) Recently Rs. 3000 for health	Rs. 50,000 for two-room housing	Rs. 450 for single room Rs. 350 for double room Rs. 250 for four per room	footnote 3
10. Madhuban (Badnera)	Rs. 1000 for death	Nil	Nil	Nil
11. Blind Women's Home, Dhayari (Pune)	Nil	Nil	Proportion from pension*	Rs. 10 given to the inmates as pocket money
12. Gurukunj (Amravati)	Nil	Nil	Nil	Nil
13. Widows Home (Pune)	Nil	Nil	Proportion from pension*	Nil

14. Navadurga (Badalapur)	Rs. 3000 for health	Rs. 65,000 for two rooms Rs. 30,000 for one room	Rs. 450	Nil
15. Chainani (Mulund)	Nil	Nil	Rs. 700	Three kinds of rooms but no distinction in food.
16. Hingane (near Pune)		Earlier Rs. 20,000, presently Rs. 30,000	Rs. 500	The old make their own arrangements for food from the premises
17. Shatayu Bhavan	10,000	Rs. 10,000	Rs. 600	Nil
18. Matrukul	1000	Nil	Rs. 450	Nil
19. Ambutai Mehendale	Nil	Nil	Rs. 400	Nil

* Pension was not always adequate. But a substantial portion was given to the institution leaving some for the incidentals of the inmates.

[1] In all the OAHs including those poor and receiving grants from the government, citizens in the neighbourhood contributed money for food to these institutions. Some families hosted sumptuous meals to mark the death or other kinds of anniversaries of the inmates. Some gave grains, some clothes and so on. The amounts to be spent on various types of food to be served to the inmates were fixed by the institutions.

[2] When a single person or couples could not afford to live alone, they sold their belongings and paid whatever cash they had to the institution. Some of the inmates sold their land in old age and lived in the institution all their remaining lives. The sums paid were therefore not fixed.

[3] In Panchavati there was no rule for payment to the institution earlier. Whoever needing shelter was given that here. The parent institution of this OAH was a big charitable hospital and it had a number of its branches in the nearby towns. A number of widows worked in them for very small salaries. In their old age some arrangements had to be made for their stay with little or no money. That is how this OAH was started. But presently its rules have been changed.

[4] In Hingane too the widows were working on a voluntary basis in the school, high school or the hostel for girls on the premises. When they retired some arrangement had to be made for their old age because they had hardly any ties with their relatives. In fact it was this stay in the premises that gave the authorities the idea of opening an OAH. Since there was a girls' hostel on the premises, any arrangement for food was possible. The old could also cook for themselves at their convenience.

only the lonely, helpless and needy live in old-age homes. This is not always true. Even when not living alone, some of the elderly perhaps felt unwanted, either because family members were too busy or there was a shortage of space. There were others who did not want to depend on their relatives but did not have the courage to live alone away from them. The aged in these situations also went to live in old-age homes. This allowed them to maintain good relations with their relatives and enjoy their company for a short while, when they occasionally visited them, without leaving the security of their old-age home.

It is clear that the longevity of the Indian population is going to increase in future. Poverty may not be alleviated quickly. Thus the need for old-age homes especially among the poor is bound to increase. It is also likely that larger numbers may be bedridden, thus escalating the demand for institutions which accept government grants. But government grants always fall short of the requirements, and old-age homes have to depend on donations from the public. While often these donations are sufficient, there are instances when these donations fall short. A case-study of an old-age home, David Sassoon's Niwara, which does more than just keep body and soul together, is described below. It tries to anticipate future developments by extending its horizons.

Started in August 1863 by a few *sardar* (feudal landlords of earlier times) families in Pune who came together to start a home for the helpless, Niwara, did not charge a single pie from the inmates who were really poor. They were interviewed at the time of entry regarding the extent of their loneliness or helplessness. Only after having established that they were really helpless, were they admitted. This category of 'helpless' was not well-defined. It could include anybody, the old, orphaned children, helpless women or mentally handicapped persons, in need of some shelter and food. Usually, a more than adequate helping (a *thali*) was given twice a day and was occasionally wasted. Sometimes it was also sold to others. This kind of arrangement continued till 1974.

Initially in 1863 the *sardars* approached David Sassoon, a Jew who was visiting Pune at that time, for funds. He immediately gifted them Rs. 25,000 and the institution was named after him. With this grant in hand, the *sardars* held a meeting and approached the public for help. People donated to the cause with great zeal. Though the records of the early years are not well-maintained, it appears the *sardar* family mentioned above maintained the David Sassoon Home for three generations. The *sardar* of the third generation approached a social worker in 1974 and requested him to take over the responsibility for the home. Modern in his approach, this social worker wanted the whole institution to be streamlined and its jurisdiction well-defined. He decided to take only men and women of 60 years of age or above into the institution and called it Niwara—a peaceful shelter. No person having a son or some close relatives to take care of him/her was admitted into the institution. The larger aim was to inculcate in society a system of good values—of families looking after their own old or destitute.

The institution was thus reorganized along modern lines after 1974. There was a fixed day in the week when those eligible were interviewed and admitted. The funds needed for the home were raised through a variety of sources. The public was approached and the cooperation of the neighbouring Rotary clubs was obtained. Generally it was found that the public was prepared to donate funds liberally in terms of cash or kind. Donations for taking care of the subsistence needs of the inmates were not lacking. Retired educated women were willing to work free for the home. Doctors were prepared to give medical help at a low cost. In addition to food, clothes, medicines, books and magazines were also donated by the public. The Rotary clubs helped build a big public hall on the premises for the inmates' use, which was also hired out for public lectures and performances to earn money for the OAH.

This OAH fortunately had a well-located, sizeable piece of land. In their leisure time the old opted for vegetable gardening. In fact, the new supervisor had got banana trees planted with the help of the healthy inmates, along with casual labour. Yielding fruit worth Rs. 200 a day for the last three years, these banana trees generated much needed income to improve the lot of the inmates.

A physiotherapy centre was started on the premises with the idea of giving the therapy to outsiders too for some reasonable charge, while allowing the old inmates to avail of this facility whenever needed.

Another institution available on the premises was the convalescent home. Outsiders could place their relatives here for Rs. 25 a day and get help at the *dai* level. Though no food was provided, tea was given. The non-availability of food posed no doubt a great problem for those wishing to avail of this service. But as already mentioned, Niwara strongly believed in encouraging people to observe the old family traditions of looking after their own old. It was of the view that the contact between the convalescents and their relatives could be strengthened through the provision of food by the latter. Very often those incurably paralyzed did not need daily medical attention and they could make use of this home. In big cities even *dai* level help is very costly and from this point of view, the convalescent home was a great help. The terminally ill also could be accommodated here. A medical specialist visited the OAH daily, and his advice could be taken for convalescent patients.

The advantages in developing the Niwara old-age home as described above were threefold. First, the relevant facilities were available to the old themselves; second, these facilities could be used by outsiders and made paying or productive; third, they facilitated the integration of the old with society at large. This helped the old to come into contact with a slightly different world on the premises, which reduced their isolation.

Thus the gradual development of different facets of the OAH helped to improve its ambience. The supervisor of Niwara wanted to raise the living standards of the inmates and that seemed a definite possibility in the not too distant future—the biggest assest of this OAH was the land it owned in land-hungry Pune city. By adding new institutions to its premises, it hoped to raise more resources.

Part II: Socio-cultural Profile of the Inmates

The inmates of the 19 OAHs were interviewed with the help of a questionnaire. As noted earlier, the inmates fell into two categories: the poor, and the relatively well-to-do who could pay Rs. 250 to Rs. 700 per month for their upkeep. Together they constituted the 541 inmates interviewed by us. Beside these there were about 30 persons who though in the homes belonged to the 55–60 age group. Another 13 were either dumb or mentally deranged and could not answer the questions in the questionnaire in a consistent manner. Twenty of the inmates were out of the home, either in the hospital or at their relatives' place, and hence could not be interviewed. The questionnaire canvassed was about 9 pages long. The information was collected under the following heads: the setting or composition of the household from which the inmate had come; the number of sons and daughters living and/or dead; the nature of the housing the inmate experienced prior to the stay in the institution; his or her belongings at that time; health and occupation when aged about 50; earlier and current earnings; monthly payment to the OAH and who made it; extent of satisfaction with life in the OAH; health and mobility; leisure activities; attitudes to old age and death.

There were 190 men and 351 women among the inmates. Thus women constituted about 65 per cent of the total inmates. The age distribution of men and women is shown in Table 4.4.

Table 4.4
Inmates of OAHs by Sex and Age Group

Age Group	Men	Women	Total
60–64	19	70	89
65–69	28	82	110
70–74	47	83	130
75–79	49	52	101
80 and above	47	64	111
Total	190	351	541

The maximum number of inmates was from the age group 70–74 years. Surprisingly the number above 80 years was also large, namely 111. This may be due to the exaggeration of ages reported by the inmates. The average age of men was 74 and of women 71.4.

Did the Old Persons Have Spouses? Where Were They?

The inmates of the OAHs were asked about their spouses. Their whereabouts as reported by them is shown in Table 4.5.

Over two-thirds, i.e., 68.4 per cent, of the old were widowed and 14.2 per cent were unmarried (a sizeable percentage). About 9 per cent had a spouse who lived away. Probably in such cases, one parent was accepted by the children while the other came to live in an OAH. In this category the majority were men. In 5.4 per cent of the cases both husband and wife lived in an OAH.

Table 4.5
Whereabouts of Spouses of the Inmates

Spouse	Men	Women	Total	Per cent
Dead	93	277	370	68.4
Alive but live away	30	18	48	8.9
Alive, living together	15	14	29	5.4
Unmarried	50	27	77	14.2
Not known	2	15	17	3.1
Total	190	351	541	100.0

The onset of widowhood is an important landmark in the lives of the old. It influences their extent of loneliness as well as their family status. The distribution of the number of years since the incidence of widowhood is presented in Table 4.6.

Table 4.6
Number of Years Since the Inmates had been Widowed

No. of Years	Men	Women	Total	Per Cent
1–3	9	22	31	8.4
4–6	12	15	27	7.3
7–9	8	21	29	7.8
10–12	10	35	45	12.2
13–15	9	18	27	7.3
16–18	5	14	19	5.1
19–21	11	16	27	7.3
21+	28	137	165	44.6
Total	92	278	370	100.0

As seen from the table, a large majority of almost 45 per cent had been widowed for over 21 years. Widowhood was a recent affair, i.e., less than 4 years, in the case of 8.4 per cent men and women.

From Where did the Inmates Come

Table 4.7 provides the answers. About 14 per cent of the inmates came from rural areas, another 36 per cent from smaller towns,

Table 4.7
Rural/Urban Distribution of the Inmates

Place Coming From	Men	Women	Total
Rural	36	41	77
Small town	78	119	197
City	76	191	267
Total	190	351	541

and the remaining, that is about 50 per cent, were from cities. Obviously the number coming from cities was large because people here were more likely to know about the OAHs. Moreover, as will be discussed later, it is a moot question whether city life forced the old to take shelter in OAHs due to the shortage of housing and other problems of urbanization.

With Whom Were the Inmates Living Earlier?

Men and women in the OAHs had left their households to come to the OAH. It was quite likely that they either did not want to depend on their relatives or had none, and getting older they preferred to live in an OAH rather than alone. The answers of the inmates are set out in Table 4.8.

Table 4.8
With Whom Were the Inmates Living Earlier?

Living with whom	Men	Women	Total	Per cent
Living alone	76	121	197	36.4
Sons or stepsons	47	85	132	24.4
Married daughter	3	23	26	4.8
Unmarried daughter	1	2	3	0.6
Spouse	20	31	51	9.4
Brother (relative from parents' side in case of women)	20	44	64	11.8
Unmarried or widowed sister	1	4	5	0.9
Married sister	5	6	11	2.0
Other relatives	9	23	32	6.0
Family not related to them	8	12	20	3.7
Total	190	351	541	100.0

A sizeable number of the inmates, to the extent of 36 per cent, had been living alone before they shifted to an old-age home. About 10 per cent were living with remotely related or unrelated people and another 9 per cent as couples. Probably with age the last-mentioned category had been widowed; lonely and with no one else to look after them, they decided to shift to an OAH. Together these three groups, comprising 55 per cent of the inmates, were most in need of the help and services of an old-age home. While 24 per cent of the inmates had been living with their sons, the latter were preparing to move them to an OAH for the following reasons: (*i*) it was difficult to look after them temperamentally; (*ii*) parents were disabled or paralyzed and nursing them was not easy; (*iii*) there was shortage of housing (for instance one woman had four sons, each living in a one-room tenement in the city—neither could accommodate a disabled person in the house); (*iv*) some of them were incompatible in nature with their parents and hence the old themselves preferred to stay in an OAH.

Daughters and sisters, married as well as single, looked after the old to the extent of 8 per cent—not a negligible number. What one would like to see is, more sisters or daughters providing shelter to the old. However it will be seen later that daughters cared a lot for their parents in old age. Brothers or parents' families also provided shelter to both men and women, more so to the latter.

What Kind of Housing Did the Inmates Have Before Coming to an OAH?

Table 4.9 provides the information summarized here. If we combine those with no shelter, hut owners and those institutionalized, we get 14 per cent that had no shelter before coming to the OAH. Another 13.5 per cent were living in somebody's house, probably free, unable to pay rent. About 25 per cent had rented room or rooms. Only about 19 per cent reported having their own house, maybe just a modest one. Another meagre 5.5 per cent reported that they lived in a relatively big house before coming to the OAH. As will be seen in Chapter 5, this pattern of accommodation of the inmates of the OAH was quite different from the housing pattern of the average elderly villager in our survey.

Table 4.9
Housing of Inmates Before Coming to OAHs

Kind of Housing	Men	Women	Total	Per Cent
No shelter	5	26	31	5.7
Hutment	7	12	19	3.5
No housing, institutionalized	12	15	27	5.0
Somebody's house	20	53	73	13.5
Rented room or rooms	45	89	134	24.8
Rented house	23	46	69	12.8
Rented flat	4	9	13	2.4
Own flat	18	25	43	7.9
Own house	45	57	102	18.9
Own big house	11	19	30	5.5
Total	190	351	541	100.0

What Was the Occupation of the Inmates Before They Entered an OAH?

The occupational distribution of men and women before coming to the OAH is shown in Table 4.10.

Table 4.10
Occupation of Inmates Before Coming to OAHs

Occupation	Men	Women	Total	Per Cent
Own household work	–	131	131	24.2
Other's household work	3	69	72	13.3
Private unskilled service	43	14	57	10.5
Private skilled service	27	26	53	9.8
Own farming	9	3	12	2.2
Agricultural labour	21	27	48	8.9
Own business	52	31	83	15.3
Unskilled job (organized sector)	19	8	27	5.0
Skilled job (organized sector)	11	17	28	5.2
Unemployed	4	9	13	2.4
Social worker	0	9	9	1.7
Nothing because well-to-do	0	7	7	1.3
Not reported	1	0	1	0.2
Total	190	351	541	100.0

Most striking is the fact that a very small number, namely 9 men and 3 women, worked on their own farms before entering an old-age home. The likely reasons for this small number are well-known. Probably they lived alone with nobody to help with the farming; often they sold the land and gave the money (whatever it was) to the OAH as in the Phirodia OAH. Or if persons owning farms had children, they clung to their land and did not care to live in an OAH. The next chapter will provide ample proof for this. It is also likely that rural folk did not know about the existence of OAHs.

Of those who had been agricultural labourers, 21 were men and 27 women. They formed less than 9 per cent of the total inmates. They probably had to join an OAH when they could no longer work for wages. More than 15 per cent were doing their own business, such as running small shops, before they moved to an OAH.

Among women, 37 per cent had taken care of domestic chores; another 20 per cent had worked in the households of others—in all, 57 per cent of the women had been engaged in housework. While only 17 women, i.e., less than 5 per cent, were working at skilled jobs in the organized sector, only 9 women and 4 men had been totally unemployed—a small number compared to the prevailing unemployment rate. Finally, only 7 women boasted of doing nothing before coming to the OAH because they were well-to-do. Thus, a large majority of men as well as women came from poorer classes. Workers from the semi-organized or the organized sector were few.

Retirement Age of the Inmates

Another area of interest was the age at which the inmates retired. When women stopped doing household work they reported that they had retired. Women sometimes stopped doing the domestic chores when a daughter-in-law started living in the house. The age of retirement is shown in Table 4.11.

Most of those still working were employed in the old-age home itself. In fact some of them had been with the institution since their younger days; after they crossed 60, they continued their work and stayed in the old-age home. A majority of those who had never worked were females from well-to-do classes. Occasionally there were cases of handicapped persons who could not work.

Table 4.11
Age of Retirement of Inmates of Old-Age Homes

Age of Retirement (Years)	Males	Females	Total	Per Cent
Never working	2	15	17	3.1
20–39	5	2	7	1.3
40–49	8	3	11	2.0
50–59	54	99	153	28.3
60–69	77	144	221	40.9
70–79	38	64	102	18.9
80–89	1	5	6	1.1
95	1	0	1	0.2
Still working	4	19	23	4.3
Total	190	351	541	100.0

Those that had retired at ages below 50 often had some disability which prevented them from working. There was a case of a person suffering from leprosy who had to retire because even though he got cured, he was not accepted by society. So after turning 60 he joined an old-age home where he got along with others despite their knowing that he had had leprosy earlier. However, he worked in the garden and never in the kitchen or inside the home.

Twenty-eight per cent had retired at ages between 50 and 59. The retirement age was considered to be as 55. Even today in certain sectors people are retired at the age of 58. Forty-one per cent retired between the ages of 60 and 69. There was also a substantial percentage (18.9) retiring even as late as 70–79.

Yearly Income of the Inmates

Data about the yearly income of the old from the vocation practised before coming to an OAH was obtained from the inmates. The income distribution of the old men and women can be seen in Table 4.12. Before moving to an OAH 40 per cent of the inmates had had an yearly income of less than Rs. 500 and another 11 per cent less than Rs. 1,000. Assuming that for two full meals a day an average of at least Rs. 960 a year is needed, about 52 per cent were living below the poverty line—i.e., even if they had no dependents, they could not maintain themselves. This was only to be expected in a country like India. Most people live from hand to mouth even when young and vigorous and they cannot dream of saving for old

Table 4.12
Yearly Income of the Old Before Coming to an OAH

Income in Rs.	Men	Women	Total	Per Cent
−500	18	201	219	40.5
501–1,000	20	42	62	11.5
1,001–2,000	33	47	80	14.8
2,001–5,000	46	26	72	13.3
6,000–10,000	27	22	49	9.1
11,000–15,000	21	9	30	5.5
16,000–20,000	10	1	11	2.0
21,000–25,000	6	2	8	1.5
Above 25,000	9	1	10	1.8
Total	190	351	541	100.0

age. In fact our rural survey in Maharashtra, reported in a later chapter, showed that people had rarely thought of saving for old age. Forty-three per cent of the old inmates probably had enough to eat if they had no dependents, which was unlikely (as discussed in the previous chapter, a sizeable percentage had dependents). But certainly they had no capacity to save for old age. Thus the picture of all-round poverty is amply clear and there is little hope that this situation will change much in the near future.

Only 5.3 per cent had had an annual income of more than Rs. 15,000. While certainly not high, this income allowed them to eat comfortably.

A corollary of the above is that the inmates of OAHs had had in their younger days a limited capacity for saving for old age. Their savings are presented in Table 4.13. Where necessary, the rate of interest has been assumed to be 12 per cent per annum on their investments.

Two-thirds of the inmates had no savings at all. Another 7.8 per cent had saved less than Rs. 10,000. Moreover, there was nobody to look after whatever little they had by way of possessions. Hence they sold their meagre assets including land, house, gold or cattle and gave that money to the OAH. One gets some idea of the extent of savings by noting that an investment of Rs. 1,000 fetches about Rs. 10 per month. Thus the upper limit of the second savings group in Table 4.12 would fetch Rs. 100 per month—just enough to feed one person per month. In other words, 76.4 per cent of the

Table 4.13
Savings of Inmates of Old-Age Homes

Savings in Rs. (Thousands)	Men	Women	Total	Per Cent
Nothing	126	245	371	68.6
–10	14	28	42	7.8
10–19	9	15	24	4.4
20–29	4	12	16	3.0
30–39	9	17	26	4.8
40–49	5	12	17	3.1
50–59	6	6	12	2.2
60–69	4	3	7	1.3
70–79	1	4	5	0.9
80–89	0	2	2	0.4
99+	12	7	19	3.5
Total	190	351	541	100.0

inmates would have just about survived if they had not come to an OAH. Only 8.3 per cent of the inmates had savings of more than Rs. 50,000 which could fetch Rs. 500 per month. This was often the amount that had to be paid to OAHs which accepted money for keeping the inmates in relative comfort.

Who Brought the Old to OAHs?

The inmates of the institutions were asked as to who brought them to the OAH. Their answers are set out in Table 4.14.

A substantial 42.3 per cent of the inmates came to the OAH on their own. Surprisingly, though small, there were six cases in which the spouse had brought the inmate to the OAH—either because the partner was disabled or temperamentally difficult. Sons or sons-in-law, daughters or daughters-in-law, brothers or sisters had each brought the inmates to the institution in 6 per cent of the cases. One-fourth of the inmates had been brought in by unrelated persons.

Reasons for Moving to OAHs

The inmates' reasons for moving to OAHs are presented in Table 4.15.

Table 4.14
Who Brought Inmates to OAHs

Person Bringing	Men	Women	Total	Per Cent
Self	95	134	229	42.3
Spouse	1	5	6	1.1
Son or son-in-law	10	17	27	5.0
Daughter or daughter-in-law	3	29	32	5.9
Brother or sister	9	25	34	6.3
Grandchild	1	4	5	0.9
Nephews	7	15	22	4.1
Other relatives	16	32	48	8.9
Unrelated person	48	90	138	25.5
Total	190	351	541	100.0

Table 4.15
Reasons for Moving to OAHs

Reason	Men	Women	Total	Per Cent
Nobody to take care	35	67	102	18.9
Nobody to care and no money	83	159	242	44.7
Difficult to accommodate	1	5	6	1.1
Disagreed with relatives, relatives too busy, relatives cheated	8	10	18	3.3
Disagreed with son	41	56	97	17.9
Housing too inadequate	5	11	16	3.0
Did not like to be dependent	14	39	53	9.8
To do social work	3	4	7	1.3
Total	190	351	541	100.0

Almost 64 per cent of the inmates had nobody to take care of them, and among these 45 per cent had no money either. Nineteen per cent were alone but money was not a stated serious problem. Of the cases in the first category (no one to take care of them) 29 out of 102 had passed the age of 80 and 46 had crossed 75 years. Therefore they had no place to go if they were alone except an OAH. Among the 242 living alone and without any money, 40 had passed the age of 80 and 76 had crossed 75 years. The percentage coming to an OAH because of differences with the son was also sizeable , namely 17.9. A not insignificant proportion, namely 9.8

per cent, did not want to depend on anybody. This category was probably from cities and the well-to-do class. Similarly the 3 per cent who reported shortage of housing might have been from cities.

Payments by Inmates to OAHs

Considering the annual income and the savings of the inmates of OAHs, they could not be expected to pay much. In some cases relatives or well-wishers paid for the inmates. The amounts paid to the OAHs by the inmates are shown in Table 4.16.

Table 4.16
Monthly Payment to Old-Age Homes

Monthly Payment (Rs.)	Men	Women	Total	Per Cent
Nothing	117	160	277	51.2
< = 100	7	18	25	4.6
101–200	8	49	57	10.5
201–300	2	14	16	3.0
301–400	15	27	42	7.8
401–500	17	52	69	12.8
501–600	10	18	28	5.2
601–700	1	3	4	0.7
More than 700	13	10	23	4.3
Total	190	351	541	100.0

More than half the inmates were paying nothing. An additional 4.6 per cent were able to pay up to Rs. 100. Very often poor pensioners ended up paying a major portion of their pensions, keeping only a small amount for their incidentals. Government grants to OAHs consisted of Rs. 100 to 125 per person[8] per month for their food and upkeep. There was some additional grant for furnishings such as beds, chests or plates. This amount was much less than required though the government had permitted the OAHs to collect donations, as mentioned in Part I of this chapter. It is estimated that a sum of at least Rs. 200 per person per month was

[8] Even here there were many stories of corruption and misappropriation of funds.

needed to maintain even a minimal standard of living, but as seen in Table 4.15, a hefty 66.3 per cent of the old paid less than this requisite amount. This is the sad part of the running of institutions. Only about 10 per cent were able to pay more than Rs. 500 per month. The comparison with the monthly charges of the OAH described in Part I is telling.

Who Paid for the Upkeep of Inmates?

Table 4.17 gives the breakdown of the various sources of payments made. It will be seen that apart from their own savings and/pensions, relatives and unrelated persons helped out. More than half were paying nothing because there was nobody to pay. Twenty per cent of the inmates paid from their savings and 10 per cent from their pensions. Thus 30 per cent could pay for themselves. Sons or sons-in-law paid for their upkeep only in 5 per cent of the cases; and daughters or daughters-in-law in 2 per cent of the cases. In the case of 3.9 per cent of the inmates, the landlords or distant relatives paid the charges of the OAH. These are included among the 39 (7.2 per cent) paid for by relatives and other sources. This was often the case where women had worked in their landlords' houses as long as they could; later they were helped by the landlords in this way who even visited them frequently.

Table 4.17
Who Paid for the Upkeep of Inmates?

Persons Paying	Men	Women	Total	Per Cent
None	115	167	282	52.1
Inmate himself/herself	40	69	109	20.1
Trust or some organization	0	1	1	0.2
Partly own, partly others	1	1	2	0.4
Inmates' property looked after by others	3	13	16	3.0
Partly relatives, partly other sources	10	29	39	7.2
Sons & sons-in-law	7	20	27	5.0
Daughters & daughters-in-law	1	10	11	2.0
Pension	13	41	54	10.0
Total	190	351	541	100.0

Visits of the Old Outside OAHs

Those staying in the OAH needed short outings occasionally. Generally, the old were not allowed to leave the home without reporting where they were going and when they were coming back. Since it was the responsibility of the home to keep the inmates safe and healthy, certain rules of the institution to ensure this had to be followed. Of course the relatives were consulted regarding the visits of the inmates outside the home. For many there was nobody outside to visit. In Table 4.18 the data on frequency of visits of the inmates to their relatives are presented.

Table 4.18
Frequency of the Outings of Inmates

Frequency	Men	Women	Total	Per Cent
Never	108	193	301	55.7
Rarely	23	55	78	14.4
Weekly	2	3	5	0.9
Monthly	27	21	48	8.9
Quarterly	23	53	76	14.0
Frequently	1	1	2	0.4
Six Monthly	6	25	31	5.7
Total	190	351	541	100.0

For almost 56 per cent of the inmates there was nobody to go to, while another 14 per cent visited relatives very rarely. Thus, about 70 per cent of the inmates, both men and women, had few interests outside the OAH. Others felt the need to keep in touch with their relatives and visited them. Living away from them, they were able to maintain a good relationship. After the visit the old returned to the security of their peers. One has to remember that the inmates in our old-age homes were rarely taken for outings, to gardens or museums or similar places as they are in the United States or other Western countries. Thus, visiting their relatives was their only outing.

Visits of Relatives to OAHs

How frequently did relatives visit the old in the old-age homes? As seen in Table 4.19 relatives' visits to the old-age homes were more frequent than the old visiting their relatives outside.

Table 4.19
Frequency of Visits of Relatives to OAHs

Frequency	Men	Women	Total	Per Cent
Never	98	104	202	37.3
Rarely	25	65	90	16.6
Weekly	5	4	9	1.7
Monthly	16	33	49	9.1
Quarterly	34	114	148	27.4
Frequently	1	1	2	0.4
Six Monthly	11	30	41	7.6
Total	190	351	541	100.0

About 11 per cent of the inmates had their relatives visiting them regularly, i.e., weekly, monthly, or frequently. Sadly, of course the largest percentage, 54, were those who rarely had any visitors. Twenty-seven per cent of the inmates had quarterly visitors—not a bad state of affairs. The situation regarding outings or relatives' visits to the old-age homes was also reflected in the answers of the inmates to the questions: Would you like to leave the old-age home? The answers are presented in Table 4.20. Among the inmates of the OAHs 63 per cent of the inmates were unwilling to leave the OAH. Another 17.4 per cent found the home satisfactory. Thus, in all 80 per cent liked the old-age home. In other words they had accepted the home as their own home. The remaining 20 per cent would rather be elsewhere but could not leave for various reasons—nowhere to go, financial constraints, felt awkward, etc Thus on the whole, it seemed that the old-age homes catered to the needs of the majority; at least the inmates were better off living in them than outside.

Medical Facilities Available to the Inmates

In what follows we describe the facilities available to the inmates in the old-age homes. Occasionally their availability before the

Table 4.20
Did Inmates Like to Leave the Old-Age Home?

Inclination to Leave the OAH	Men	Women	Total	Per Cent
Not willing	125	216	341	63.0
Would like to but lack adequate response from family	5	20	25	4.6
Nowhere to go	19	34	53	9.8
Would like to go but no money	1	2	3	0.6
OAH is satisfactory	36	58	94	17.4
Will go depending on the conditions at home or the response of certain persons there	4	15	19	3.5
Would like to go but feel awkward	0	6	6	1.1
Total	190	351	541	100.0

inmates had moved to OAHs was also enquired into. For instance, inmates were asked whether they had got medical help before they started living in old-age homes. The data are presented in Table 4.21.

Table 4.21
Medical Help Available to Inmates Before Coming to OAHs

Availability of Medical Help	Men	Women	Total	Per Cent
Never got help	16	28	44	8.1
Did not need nor could afford	26	33	59	10.9
Much better help earlier	5	4	9	1.7
Not needed but could afford	20	34	54	10.0
Got it when needed	123	252	375	69.3
Total	190	351	541	100.0

About 69.3 per cent of the inmates had got medical help whenever needed before they joined the home. Another 10 per cent reported that they had not needed help but could afford it. Thus 80 per cent had had no problem in getting medical help earlier. Another 1.7 per cent were probably not happy with the help they got in the old-age home because they reported that the help available prior to joining was better. Nineteen per cent constituted those that did not get help earlier—11 per cent reporting that they

could neither afford it nor needed it, while 8 per cent said they never got the help.

The medical help availed of in the OAHs was classified according to the frequency with which it was needed by the inmates. The relevant data are presented in Table 4.22.

Table 4.22
Medical Help Needed by the Inmates

Frequency of Medical Help Needed	Men	Women	Total	Per Cent
Never needed	46	55	101	18.7
Rarely needed	54	112	166	30.7
Once a week	2	5	7	1.3
Once a month	6	12	18	3.3
Once in 2 to 3 months	19	40	59	10.9
Constantly needed	63	127	190	35.1
Total	190	351	541	100.0

About half the inmates, i.e., 49.4 per cent, did not need or rarely needed any medical help. A little more than one-third, i.e., 35.1 per cent, needed to be attended to regularly. They were probably patients suffering from asthma, diabetes, blood pressure or other diseases requiring constant medication.

Mobility of the Inmates

As can be seen from Table 4.23, about 8 per cent of the inmates had limited mobility. They included the 4.4 per cent who were bedridden and the 3.4 per cent whose mobility was restricted because of blindness. While 35 per cent were slightly mobile, more than half, i.e., 54.7 per cent, were quite mobile. It was this last category which suggested that the old were satisfactorily placed in OAHs.

The age distribution of those who were (a) bedridden and (b) slightly mobile and the percentage in each age group is shown in Table 4.24. It is clear that mobility decreased with age for both men and women.

Table 4.23
Mobility of the Inmates of OAHs

Mobility	Men	Women	Total	Per Cent
Bedridden	7	17	24	4.4
Slightly mobile	63	127	190	35.1
Fairly mobile	67	138	205	37.9
Quite mobile	46	45	91	16.8
Mobility with wheelchair	0	2	2	0.4
Mobility with a stick	6	5	11	2.0
Limited mobility because of blindness	1	17	18	3.3
Total	190	351	541	100.0

Table 4.24
Age Distribution of (a) Bedridden and (b) Slightly Mobile in OAHs

Age Group	Men				Women			
	(a)	(b)	% of a & b	Total in Age Group	(a)	(b)	% of a & b	Total in Age Group
60–64	1	4	26.3	19	2	13	21.4	70
65–69	0	7	25.0	28	4	23	33.0	82
70–74	0	14	30.0	47	2	30	38.6	83
75–79	3	16	38.8	49	2	22	46.2	52
80 & above	3	22	53.2	47	7	39	71.9	64
Total	7	63	36.8	190	17	127	41.0	351

Health Complaints of the Inmates

The inmates of the OAH were asked about their health troubles. Some of them had more than two ailments to report. But we chose for purpose of classification in this study only the two most serious ones. In other words, when up to two ailments were reported, both were included in the present analysis. But when more than two were mentioned, the relatively minor ailments were dropped. The findings are exhibited in Table 4.25.

Sixty-four inmates, i.e., 11.8 per cent did not have a single complaint regarding their health. Another 32.9 per cent mentioned

Table 4.25
Health Complaints of the Inmates of Old-Age Homes

Complaints	Men	Women	Total	Per Cent
No complaint	15	49	64	11.8
Only one complaint	59	119	178	32.9
Diabetes	9	27	36	6.7
Paralysis	8	18	26	4.8
Asthma	25	21	46	8.5
Cough	7	13	20	3.7
Tuberculosis	2	3	5	0.9
Heart disease	15	25	40	7.4
Blood pressure	22	67	89	16.4
Forgetfulness	0	3	3	0.5
Kidney trouble	17	5	22	4.1
Tremor	10	11	21	3.9
Arthritis	8	37	45	8.3
Rheumatism	27	39	66	12.2
Cataract	33	40	73	13.5
Eye defects	34	53	87	16.1
Deafness	19	17	36	6.7
Mentally confused	3	5	8	1.5
Anaemia	24	65	89	16.4
Giddiness	1	4	5	0.9
Blindness	8	22	30	5.5
Disabilities of arms and legs	11	18	29	5.4
Psychic troubles	8	16	24	4.4
Fits	0	7	7	1.3
Varicose veins	1	1	2	0.4
Leprosy	0	2	2	0.4
Speech defect	0	4	4	0.7
Benumbing of senses	1	2	3	0.5
Fever	2	4	6	1.1
Skin disease	1	1	2	0.4
Stomach complaints	0	2	2	0.4
Cancer	1	1	2	0.4
Gynaecological trouble	0	2	2	0.4
More than two serious diseases	4	3	7	1.3

Note: Total cannot be given because of multiple complaints.

just one complaint. Others had reported two or more complaints. Diabetes was reported by 6.7 per cent and paralysis by 4.8 per cent. The problem of the latter group was particularly serious because it totally incapacitated the inmates, preventing them from moving freely. Asthma troubled 8.5 per cent and heart disease 7.4

per cent of the inmates. Blood pressure, anaemia and eye defects were complained of by 16 per cent each. Seven cases reported more than two serious troubles.

Personal Help Needed by the Inmates

On the whole the inmates were neither unhealthy nor bedridden to the extent of needing help for everyday living. Most of them carried on without help as seen in Table 4.26 given below.

Table 4.26
Personal Help Needed for Everyday Living

Help Needed	Men	Women	Total	Per Cent
No need	174 (91.6%)	286 (81.5%)	460	85.0
Needed help for everything	8	12	20	3.7
Needed help to go to latrine	1	2	3	0.6
Needed help to get dressed	0	3	3	0.6
Help for going outside	4	21	25	4.6
Help for washing clothes and utensils	3	27	30	5.5
Total	190	351	541	100.0

Fortunately 85 per cent of the inmates of the institutions did not need any help whatsoever. Males were more independent in terms of mobility than women. Twenty inmates, i.e., 3.7 per cent, needed help for everything. Some inmates, comprising 4.6 per cent, needed help only for going outside. More than 5 per cent needed help for washing clothes or their utensils. In an old-age home like Shatayu Bhavan, 30 out of 44 persons had these chores done on payment, while the rest enjoyed doing them on their own. The former are not counted as unable to do the chores.

The inmates on the whole seemed to enjoy their stay in the old-age homes.

Tasks Performed by the Inmates

Most of the inmates were mobile and capable of doing some work. Except in a few old-age homes where they were paying Rs. 250 or more per person, they were expected to work. The kinds of tasks performed by the inmates are presented in Table 4.27.

Table 4.27
Chores the Inmates Did in Old-Age Homes

Kind of Chores	Men	Women	Total	Per Cent
Nothing	131	215	346	64.0
Kitchen chores other than cooking	5	76	81	15.0
Cooking	0	13	13	2.4
Gardening & farming	9	1	10	1.8
Sweeping	10	11	21	3.9
Marketing	5	0	5	0.9
Helping others	9	8	17	3.1
Work in the institution	9	10	19	3.5
Any work asked to do	12	17	29	5.4
Total	190	351	541	100.0

Sixty-four per cent of the inmates did none of the chores needed to run the old-age homes. The rest worked in a variety of ways. Women were more helpful, with 39 per cent of them against 31 per cent of the men doing some work for the old-age homes.

Did the Inmates Have Any Friends in the OAH?

Table 4.28
Friendships of the Inmates in Old-Age Homes

Number of and Need for Friends	Men	Women	Total	Per Cent
None	29	58	87	16.1
Loves to be alone	10	16	26	4.8
Does not like anybody	2	4	6	1.1
Quarrels with everybody	1	2	3	0.6
One or two friends	16	46	62	11.5
Three to nine friends	36	63	99	18.3
Healthy relations with all	72	114	186	34.3
Ten to twenty friends	24	48	72	13.3
Total	190	351	541	100.0

About two-thirds of the inmates, i.e., the last three rows in Table 4.28, were friendly with almost everybody. Very often all the persons housed in the same room were reported as friends. Sixteen per cent had no friends at all. About 5 per cent reported that they liked to be alone. The remaining 1.7 per cent either did not like anybody or quarrelled with everybody.

How Did the Inmates Spend Their Leisure Time?

Table 4.29
Leisure-time Activities of the Inmates of OAHs

Activity	Men	Women	Total	Per Cent
Do nothing nor are capable of doing	10	36	46	8.5
Do nothing though capable	11	15	26	4.8
Reading	32	30	62	11.5
Listening to the radio	5	10	15	2.8
Watching television	21	27	48	8.9
Writing letters	0	1	1	0.2
Meditation, yoga, *japa* (repetition of God's name and devotion to God)	38	70	108	20.0
Religious activities	16	21	37	6.8
Work in the institution	3	18	21	3.9
Radio, TV, reading	46	116	162	29.9
Playing cards or knitting	4	6	10	1.8
Own business	1	1	2	0.4
Walking	3	0	3	0.6
Total	190	351	541	100.0

About 30 per cent inmates reported that they watched TV, listened to the radio, or read in their leisure time. Another 9 per cent only watched TV and 11 per cent exclusively read in their spare time. A large percentage, 20, spent their time in meditation or *japa*, and another 6.8 per cent in religious activities. Thus, it seemed that about 27 per cent of the inmates were religious. Two persons were allowed to do their business—a woman who used to go out once a week to teach bhajans to outsiders and earn some money; and a male inmate who performed pujas (religious ceremonies) when invited.

Library Facilities Available and the Response of the Inmates

As can be seen from Table 4.30 nearly half the inmates, 47 per cent were not concerned with the library because either they could not read or were blind. Thirty per cent of the inmates reported having some reading material in the old-age home. Among them 17.9 per cent had access to a proper library and 12 per cent to only newspapers and magazines.

Table 4.30
Availability of Library Facilities

Kind of Library	Men	Women	Total	Per Cent
No library	43	30	73	13.5
Only old books given by sympathizers	15	13	28	5.2
Proper library	23	74	97	17.9
Only newspapers and Magazines available	36	29	65	12.0
Sympathizers brought books from outside	7	16	23	4.3
Not concerned with library	66	189	255	47.1
Total	190	351	541	100.0

Finally 5.2 per cent of the inmates complained that sympathizers only gave those books to the library which they wanted to dispose of. They were often not readable.

Suggestions for Improving OAHs

The inmates were asked whether they had any suggestions for improving the working of the OAHs. Many of the inmates living free or almost free felt embarrassed about voicing suggestions. They wondered what right had they to make suggestions when they were living at somebody else's cost. They did not know that today one can avail of state benefits and still have some say in what these ought to be. Their answers are given in Table 4.31.

About 80 per cent of the inmates had no complaints. This included 11.5 per cent who thought that the conditions in the home were perfect and 69 per cent who had no suggestions to make. Suggestions for improvement in the supervision often came from homes where there were paying inmates, who were of the view that better supervision would improve the facilities they had.

Table 4.31
Suggestions Made by Inmates for Improving OAHs

Suggestions	Men	Women	Total	Per Cent
No suggestions	137	237	374	69.1
Everything is satisfactory	13	49	62	11.5
Suggestions regarding bedridden patients	2	2	4	0.7
Concerning food	8	16	24	4.4
Concerning medication	13	14	27	5.0
Concerning housing	8	11	19	3.5
Furnishings for individual	0	1	1	0.2
Concerning library	1	0	1	0.2
Regarding supervision	8	21	29	5.4
Total	190	351	541	100.0

Those suggesting improvement in the food i.e., 4.4 per cent, included two kinds of groups. First, non-Maharashtrians who complained that the food was always cooked in Maharashtrian style. The second category was of the view that the food should be cooked keeping in mind the needs of old persons. For instance the rice should be soft enough for them to eat. Four inmates wanted the bedridden inmates to be kept separately from others. In some old-age homes they were kept along with others so that they did not feel isolated, and also because the healthy inmates could look after their needs. Some 27 inmates suggested that the medical stock of the hospital be improved since they could not always get the needed medicines on the premises. Another 19 thought that the housing of the inmates had scope for improvement—ceilings should not leak and too many persons should not be kept in one room. This last suggestion was especially valid since the living arrangements were not always satisfactory. Sometimes too many persons especially women, were housed in one big room, as revealed in Table 4.32.

It seems clear from Table 4.31 that too many were kept in one big room such as a dormitory. Not everybody liked it. One-fourth had either a single or double room.

Satisfaction with Life in OAHs

It is amply clear by now that the majority of inmates in old-age homes were satisfied with their conditions. The answers to a direct

Table 4.32
Living Arrangements of the Inmates

Living Arrangement	Men	Women	Total	Per Cent
Separate room	10	40	50	9.2
2 in a room	35	49	84	15.5
3 in a room	71	92	163	30.1
6–10 in a room	55	82	137	25.3
11–20 in a room	17	55	72	13.3
More than 21 together	1	27	28	5.2
Two rooms for 1	1	6	7	1.3
Total	190	351	541	100.0

question on how far they were satisfied with life in OAHs are
analyzed in Table. 4.33.

Table 4.33
Satisfaction With Life in Old-Age Homes

Satisfactory Level	Men	Women	Total	Per Cent
Fully satisfied	157	282	439	81,1
No satisfaction at all	10	15	25	4.6
Partially satisfied but have no choice	18	46	64	11.8
No complaint about home but other personal problems	5	8	13	2.4
Total	190	351	541	100.0

A large majority, 81 per cent, were fully satisfied with the
conditions in old-age homes. About 12 per cent were only partially
satisfied but had no choice. Another 4.6 per cent were thoroughly
dissatisfied with the home. Thirteen inmates, i.e., 2.4 per cent,
had no complaints about the old-age home but had other problems,
such as their own families worrying them.

Comparison of Life in an OAH with the Past

When the inmates were asked to compare their present life with
the past, a large majority felt that the earlier life had been better.

The reasons given for this feeling differed but the past seemed brighter, as is revealed in Table 4.34.

Table 4.34
Comparison of Present Life With the Past

Comparison	Men	Women	Total	Per Cent
No change	32	102	134	24.8
Both are not good	5	4	9	1.7
Present life is better	16	52	68	12.6
Earlier was much better, busier	17	21	38	7.0
Earlier better financially	12	5	17	3.1
Earlier better for health	13	32	45	8.3
Living among own people and hence better	7	39	46	8.5
Earlier was best	20	32	52	9.6
Earlier was more free	23	22	45	8.3
Cannot say	45	42	87	16.1
Total	190	351	541	100.0

It seems that a large majority who had expressed satisfaction with old-age homes, in replies to questions tabulated earlier, had done so because of the force of circumstances. As there was no other option they expressed satisfaction. But when it came to comparisons with their past, the inmates certainly felt differently. Only 12.6 per cent thought their present life an improvement. About 25 per cent saw no change in their lives—probably it had been all drudgery and so was the present. Nine of the inmates (1.7 per cent) specifically expressed that both the past and the present were no good. Sixteen per cent could not say which place was better. A sizeable 45 per cent considered their past to be better than the present.

Care from Sons and Daughters

There is an impression that only the old who have no children come to live in OAHs. But this is not always true—almost half the inmates had children. They were asked about their sons and daughters, and how far they had cared for the parents. The answers are set out in Table 4.35.

Table 4.35
Care of Inmates by Sons and Daughters

Care Taken	Men	Women	Total	Per Cent
Had only sons and they took care	5	21	26	4.8
Had only sons but they did not care	7	22	29	5.4
Had only daughters and they took care	14	47	61	11.3
Had only daughters and they did not care	11	4	15	2.8
Sons and daughters and both took care	9	35	44	8.1
Sons and daughters and both did not care	31	11	42	7.8
Sons and daughters but only sons cared	4	6	10	1.8
Sons and daughters but only daughters cared	9	19	28	5.2
No Children	96	182	278	51.4
Both children but parents keep away	4	4	8	1.5
Total	190	351	541	100.0

Half the inmates had no children, hence they could not respond to questions regarding children and the care they offered to the parents. Thirty-one per cent of the inmates had children—male, female or both—who cared for them. However, it is worth noting that it were the daughters who cared more for the parents. This observation is very significant because parents in India often care more for their sons. The finding that the daughters cared more should be borne in mind by those parents in India who prefer male children to female ones. Eight inmates had decided on their own to live away from their children. These were from an upper-middle class background and could afford to pay for their stay in the old-age homes. However, they were mostly inmates of OAHs like Shatayu Bhavan which refused to take care of the old if they fell ill, as noted earlier. A crucial question this raises is that when the inmates fall ill, can they afford to live away from their children? Once the children have got used to living without their parents, will they easily accept them in old age or when they are bedridden? In our view staying in homes like Shatayu Bhavan does not solve the problem of dependence of the ailing old, it merely defers it.

Good Things about Old Age

Generally old people are assumed to be unhappy because they have health problems. Another assumption is that recalling a happier past makes them feel sad about their present condition. But the interviews with the inmates showed that they had reasons to be happy even in old age. They were asked about what they enjoyed in old age and their answers are analyzed in Table 4.36.

Table 4.36
Good Things about Old Age

Good Things	Men	Women	Total	Per Cent
No responsibility	8	21	29	5.3
Proximity of children & grandchildren	2	3	5	0.9
Enough time for hobby and prayer	43	105	148	27.4
Approaching death	14	48	62	11.5
Many good things such as no responsibility, proximity of children and free time	8	11	19	3.5
Disengagement with life	0	3	3	0.6
Cannot say	30	107	137	25.3
Nothing good	85	53	138	25.5
Total	190	351	541	100.0

There were 48.6 per cent who were reportedly happy in old age for reasons such as no responsibility, time for hobbies and prayer, proximity of children, or even approaching of death. In fact, some of the inmates, 11.5 per cent, accepted death as a natural culmination of the course of life, of which they were not afraid. In spite of the fact that they were living in old-age homes, the inmates did not forget to mention proximity of children as a solace in old age. About one-fourth of them found nothing good in old age. They were probably fed up with their lives. Finally, 25.3 per cent of the inmates had nothing to say on this matter.

Unpleasant Aspects of Old Age

Among the things the inmates disliked about old age were separation from children and grandchildren, bad health, fear of death, dependence on children, and nobody to look after them. The frequency with which these unpleasant aspects were mentioned is presented in Table 4.37.

About 25 per cent of the cases could not think of the bad side. One may recall that a similar percentage could not mention the

Table 4.37
Aspects of Old Age Which Inmates found Unpleasant

Bad Things	Men	Women	Total	Per Cent
Children and grandchildren away	3	11	14	2.6
Bad health	9	17	26	4.8
Fear of death	2	13	15	2.8
Dependence on others	27	77	104	19.2
None to take care	19	29	48	8.9
Nothing bad, it is a natural course	27	82	109	20.1
Bad health, fear of death, dependence on others, etc.	71	19	90	16.6
Family members cannot understand the old	1	0	1	0.2
Cannot say	31	103	134	24.8
Total	190	351	541	100.0

good things about old age too. In other words, one-fourth of the inmates offered no response to such questions. It is worth noting that 20 per cent of the inmates reported that old age was a natural course which was not to be feared or resisted. A sizeable percentage (36) disliked old age because of their dependence on others. Another 9 per cent were sorry that they had nobody to take care of them. These were obviously childless and were unhappy about it.

The Number of Years in an OAH

On the whole most of the inmates had had prior troubles which they had either forgotten or accepted as a result of their stay in OAHs for substantially long periods. In Table 4.38, the number of years the old had spent in homes is given.

About 13 per cent of the inmates had been in OAHs for more than 10 years and about 19 per cent for 6 to 10 years. Thus one-third of the inmates had been in OAHs for more than 5 years.

To conclude the discussion on OAHs in Maharashtra one must remember that nobody likes to leave his or her home and live in an institution. The first choice therefore is always one's own home. But sometimes circumstances compel one to choose the second best option. In that case our OAHs were a good substitute.

In the nursing homes of the rich countries the main problem of the old is health. This cannot be easily had after the age of 80 or

Table 4.38
Number of Years the Inmates Were in OAHs

No. of Years	Total	Percentage
1	144	26.6
2	69	12.8
3	74	13.7
4	41	7.6
5	41	7.6
6–10	101	18.7
11–15	43	7.9
16–20	16	2.9
21–30	5	0.9
30+	7	1.3
Total	541	100.0

85. Few aids can give relief to the ailing old at this stage. In a poor country like India, the main problem is one of subsistence when one is too old to earn. Once the basic needs of the elderly are taken care of, they are even ready to make themselves useful to others to the extent possible. The case-studies presented in the final chapter reveal this. The OAHs in Maharashtra, therefore, present a picture of useful institutions badly needed for the homeless, helpless or childless.

5

The Rural Old in Maharashtra

The situation of the old living in rural areas is likely to differ from those based in urban centres. With the budget we had, it was difficult to enquire into the conditions of the old in big cities, given the cost of transportation. In big cities the old are likely to face problems of housing and overcrowding. Though a few city surveys had been done, their findings might not be reliable, based as they were on sampling techniques which omitted some sections of urban society. In any case, rural areas have been mostly ignored and we decided to study a sample of villagers from eight villages in four subdivisions of Maharashtra to try and find out their old-age problems if any.

A questionnaire was designed to enquire into the problems of the old in rural areas. The subjects dealt with in the questionnaire included: socio-economic setting of the old; their household composition; the children and their setting such as occupation, income etc; housing, economic conditions including data on land, cattle and poultry; their present occupation and the occupation followed when 50 years old or so; whether work load reduced with age; savings made for old age; ideas regarding retirement or pension; participation in household work; adequacy of food; health troubles now or in the past; respect from children, attitudes to death, and activities in old age.

Considering the lifestyle and mindset of the villagers, some questions seemed out of place. For instance, some villagers laughed when they were asked whether they had made any provision for old age. They so rarely earned anything more than the bare minimum that they never thought of saving, especially for their old age. They could, if at all, think of spending on the marriage and education of their children but never on themselves.

The rural areas we surveyed seemed virtually untouched by industrialization, a society primitive to a degree. Several villages were without schools. A neighbouring village might have one up to the fourth or may be seventh standard. The same was the case with medical facilities. Sometimes these facilities were available at a distance of 10 miles or more from the village. Often there was not even a post office. A bus might be available for transport, but it stopped a couple of miles away from the village.

Of the 35,000 odd villages in the state of Maharashtra, eight were selected for our survey—two from each of the four subdivisions of Maharashtra. Convenience of approach was the main consideration in selecting them. From the eight villages selected, a total of 601 old persons were interviewed (see Table 5.1).

Table 5.1
Villages in Maharashtra Selected for Enquiry

Subdivision	Names of Villages	No. of Old Interviewed	Total Interviewed in the Subdivision
Konkan	a) Kalethar	76	127
	b) Madh	51	
Marathwada	a) Budhoda	50	148
	b) Bhatkheda	98	
Vidarbha	a) Dabha	70	189
	b) Patansavangi	119	
West Maharashtra	a) Sangavi	65	137
	b) Savardare	72	
Total		601	601

There were 33 old persons who were not prepared to answer the questionnaire. They were mostly well-to-do, who thought that they needed no help from the government, and hence did not care to answer questions on retirement, old-age pensions or old-age homes.

The socio-economic profile of the villages is described in the following sections in order to understand the villagers' responses to our questionnaire on problems of old age.

The Rural Setting

Sangavi Village

Sangavi in Satara district is one mile away from the national highway between Pune and Satara. To reach this village one had to get down at Shirval on the highway and walk for 3 miles or avail of private jeep services. Sangavi has about 120 households. The villagers used water from the stream for drinking and washing, four or five years prior to our survey. Now, the village has piped water supplied from a public hydrant. Every household does not have piped water.

There is a primary school in the village, but for further education the children go to a neighbouring village, Naigaon. There is no medical practitioner in the village. To avail these facilities and treatment, the villagers need to go to Shirval 2.5 to 3 miles away from the village. For more serious illnesses or for surgery, the villagers have to go to Pune which is 30 miles from the village.

Sangavi is relatively prosperous because it has fairly adequate rainfall. It has some sizable land irrigated from a small dam on the stream nearby. So both rabi and kharif crops as well as vegetables are grown in this village and sold in nearby markets or in Pune. The village therefore has very few poor people. The men work in Bombay or Pune and the young women look after the agricultural operations in the village.

This village has no post office—only a postbox from where the postman of a neighbouring village collects the letters. The incoming mail is distributed either by him or the students of the school.

Modernization is beginning to make inroads into Sangavi and people are buying land on the highway for Rs.15,000 to 50,000 an acre. Some villagers have sold their land and built new houses for themselves; others have bought trucks and carry on a transport business. This village has been electrified.

Ten to fifteen years ago, some villagers used to go to Bombay to work in the textile mills; but now more are working as drivers. On the whole this village is doing well financially, probably responsible for the common perception that moving to an OAH amounts to going to a beggar's home. Thus, the thought of staying in an OAH was furthest from their minds.

Savardare Village

Savardare is in the Bhor taluka of Pune district. It has about 120 households and 75 old persons, of whom we interviewed 72. This village is 2 miles from Sarole where there is a bus stop. People have to walk from Sarole to Savardare. The taluka town Bhor is 10 miles from this village.

Savardare also has no post office, only a postbox. The village mail is gathered in this box and collected by the postman from Sarole. While there is a primary school in the village, for further education children have to travel 2 miles to Sarole.

There is one public well near the village which was used by the villagers for procuring drinking water. In summer this well would dry up and the villagers had to get water from a farm well half a mile away; but in the last 2 to 3 years since the survey, the village began getting piped water. However, it is not available in each household. There is a common area where three to four water pipes have been fixed for the convenience of the villagers.

There is no medical practitioner in the village and the villagers have to go to Bhor, 10 miles away, or to Pune, 32 miles away, for medical help. Strangely enough, this village has two bonesetters who cater to the needs of about 50 villages near about.

Savardare gets adequate rain during the monsoon but does not have much irrigated land. In the rainy season rice is cultivated and during the rest of the year, wheat, gram or unirrigated crops are grown.

Savardare is not closely connected with industry, but the villagers find employment in a Garware factory or paper-mill in a nearby village, Sarole. Previously, they used to go to Bombay to work in textile mills; but now some go to Pune as rickshaw drivers. Some own the rickshaws while others work on contract with the owners. Most villagers have some land in the village; the older people looked after the land and the younger ones worked in Bombay or Pune.

The young look after and take care of their old, and the social pressures to do so is well-recognized. Hence the old do not seem to have any problems and life goes on smoothly for them.

Kalethar Village

Kalethar is in the Malvan taluka of the coastal district of Sindhu-durg. Tarkarli, a sizable village, is 3 miles away from Kalethar; Malvan the taluka town is 5 miles away. Kalethar is a typical Konkani village, with Tarkarli as a small tourist centre on the seacoast.

Kalethar has 110 households with a population of 420 of which 76 are old persons. Most of the productive adults work in Bombay and their old live in Kalethar on remittances sent by them.

The housing in Kalethar is typical of Konkan: a modest house in the midst of a small plot of land (from 5 gunthas to 1 acre) surrounded by coconut palm trees, with a well on the premises. The neighbouring house is separated by a compound. The well water is used for drinking as well as watering the palms. During the rainy season there is ample rain, and generally there is no shortage of water.

There is a school in the village up to the seventh standard employing three teachers. For further education, students go to Malvan. There is no post office. The postman from Tarkarli comes to the village and collects letters from the postbox. There is no doctor either so villagers have to go to Tarkarli or Malvan for medical help. They are mostly rice- and fish-eating people.

There is no industrial development of any kind in Kalethar; even for marketing, villagers have to go to Malvan. From 1980 electricity has been available in the village.

The men working as casual labourers earn Rs. 20 a day and women Rs. 10–15 a day.

The people of Kalethar are just about literate. They retire quite young, around 50–55, even if keeping good health and not suffering from any serious illness.

Madh Village

Madh, in Khalapur taluka of Raigad district, is 2 miles away from Khalapur and 4 miles from Khopoli. While the former town is a mile away from Bombay–Pune road, the latter is on the road itself. This village has a well-known Ganesh temple, one among the eight accepted ones (called Ashtavinayakas). On certain days of the week, especially Fridays and Saturdays, there are many visitors to this village. In fact, the whole economy of this village depends on this temple.

The village school teaches children up to the fourth standard, after which they go to school in Khalapur or Khopoli. The villagers come here for medical help as well since Madh has no doctor.

For drinking water some well-to-do persons have wells on their own home premises. Madh has four public wells near a pond in the village.

There is ample rain in the rainy season and rice is the main crop, but the village has no irrigated land at all and hence no rabi crop. Not much of village produce is marketed; most of it is consumed locally. There is no industry nearby except in Khopoli, where young adults go to work. A weekly bazar is held, both in Khopoli and Khalapur. The village has had electricity for the last 15 years.

Bhatkheda Village

Bhatkheda is a poor village in Latur taluka of Latur district. It has a population of 1,281 (1981 census) and 219 households. There are probably 108 old people in the village, of whom 98 were interviewed by us. It has a primary as well as a high school. A medical doctor is available 10 miles away. The post office is at a distance of 5 miles, and the market village 10 miles away. Though the population of Bhatkheda is more than a thousand, it is not very developed because of its location in a backward region.

Wheat and jowar are grown in this village. The people rarely gave details of any land they had. They are mostly illiterate. The family planning movement does not seem to have reached Bhatkheda. Deaths among children appear to be frequent. People rarely plan for old age. They argue, 'We never have enough for the present. How could we think of saving for old age? What will we eat when we stop working?'

Budhoda Village

Budhoda is located in the Ausa tahsil of Osmanabad district. According to the 1981 census, there were 320 households with a population of 1,810 persons. Every fourth household in the village list was surveyed, and 50 aged persons were interviewed.

This village has a primary and middle school. A doctor and the market village are available 5 miles away. Budhoda has a post office as well as a bus service. Electricity has reached this village. People eat the wheat and jowar which are grown locally. This village is also located in a backward region.

Patansavangi Village

Patansavangi, located in the taluka Savner of Nagpur district, has about 1,168 households and a population of 6,310 according to the 1981 census. In fact this was the biggest village surveyed by us. There were probably more than 600 old people living there. Every sixth household was surveyed and 119 aged persons were interviewed. Rather than giving details about the village, its schools or its economy, the investigator recorded the extent of satisfaction of the old with their present situation and their attitudes to OAHs.

She wrote: 'About 5 per cent of the old were prepared to go to an OAH from this village. If the OAH were located in this village itself, 15 per cent would be prepared to go to it. Most of the old villagers were living happily in their households. About 25 per cent were not so happy because they were depending on others for food or other needs. Even if they were not always treated with respect, they were not prepared to leave their sons. Ten per cent of the old were prepared to live in an OAH if they could get food and tea without working. About 5 per cent were prepared to work in the OAH if they were offered tea and food.'

The villagers often suspected that the OAH was a beggars' home. So some of them said that they were prepared to go to an OAH if its living standard was better than that of a beggar's home.

The inhabitants of Patansavangi wanted a library in their village where the old could get newspapers or magazines and books to read.

The elderly in this village also suggested that the government should give pensions to the old rather than spend money on opening OAHs. This would allow them to continue living in their own homes without being a financial burden on the family. They would be better equipped to handle the problems of old age.

About 15 old persons in Patansavangi did not allow our investigator to interview them. They declined because they were of the view that they did not need any help from the government. The sarpanch thought that a sizable number of the old would prefer to stay in the OAH if one was opened in their village.

Patansavangi had all the amenities expected in a large village: primary, middle and high schools, adequate medical facilities, including a family planning centre and a health centre with a doctor, and a post and telegraph office. Tuesday was its market day. Savner town was 14 miles away.

Dabha Village

Dabha, located in Nagpur tahsil, has a population of 503 persons and 103 households according to the 1981 census. It is 32 miles from Nagpur city. We interviewed 70 aged persons in this village.

This village has no medical centre, post office, or a weekly market day. To avail of any of these facilities, the people have to travel a distance of 5 to 10 miles. Fortunately the villagers have a potable water supply. Dabha has only a primary school. For their further education the village children had to go to a village 4 to 5 miles away to which there is a bus service.

About 7 or 8 old persons in Dabha refused to be interviewed. Mostly well-to-do, they were not looking for any help from the government and did not feel the need to respond to our questionnaire. Many agriculturists did not give any information about their landholdings. Generally, people did not like the idea of an OAH and had not thought of sending anybody there. They also felt that the government, rather than taking care of the old, should give employment to the young. People also did not like to answer questions about their children who had died. They could not understand why our enquiry included questions on deceased children.

Thus, it seemed that the eight villages selected by us were virtually undeveloped. They had not heard of old-age pensions or retirement ages and most assumed that OAHs were for beggars. Hence they preferred to live in their home village and were prepared to depend on it for their upkeep if required in their old age. On the whole, they seemed confident that the village would look after them if the need arose.

Profile of the Rural Old

In what follows the results of the 601 interviews with the old are presented to give an idea of the make-up of the elderly, the problems they faced, and how they tackled them.

Marital Status of the Elderly Villagers

Among the 601 old people interviewed, 280 were men and 321 women. They were asked about their marital status. As usual among the old men, more than three-fourths (78 per cent) were currently married, and among the women, about two-thirds were widowed. In Table 5.2 the marital status of the old is set out.

Table 5.2
Marital Status of the Elderly Villagers

Marital Status	Men	Women	Total	Per Cent
Unmarried	5	1	6	1.0
Married with partner	219	102	321	53.4
Divorced	1	3	4	0.7
Separated	5	3	8	1.3
Widowed	50	212	262	43.6
Total	280	321	601	100.0

Thus, a majority of the old were married or widowed. Two per cent were divorced or separated, and 1 per cent were unmarried. Widowhood among old women was common (66 per cent), and they would have been helpless anywhere else because they were mostly not earning. However, in the village set-up they were neither lonely nor left on their own to face problems of old age.

Present Occupation of the Elderly

The present occupations of the old were analyzed, as shown in Table 5.3. One may note that more than half the old were still working.

About 46 per cent of the old did not work. Among women, including those begging, 50 per cent and among men, 42 per cent

Table 5.3
Present Occupation of the Rural Old

Occupation	Men	Men Per-centage	Women	Women Per-centage	Total	Per Cent
Own household work	3	1.1	53	16.5	56	9.3
Other's household work	0	–	4	1.2	4	0.7
Unskilled private service	9	3.2	3	0.9	12	2.0
Skilled private service	4	1.4	0	–	4	0.7
Own farming, business and labour	65	23.2	46	14.3	111	18.5
Agricultural labour	49	17.5	47	14.6	96	16.0
Own business	14	5.0	1	0.3	15	2.5
Unskilled job in the organized sector	2	0.7	1	0.3	3	0.5
Skilled job in the organized sector	1	0.4	0	–	1	0.2
Own shop	–	–	2	0.6	2	0.3
Look after own cattle	15	5.4	0	–	15	2.5
Social work	1	0.4	1	0.3	2	0.3
Not working	117	41.8	159	49.5	276	45.9
Begging	–	–	4	1.2	4	0.7
Total	280	100.0	321	100.0	601	100.0

did not work. Thus, women formed a larger percentage of those not working. As we have seen elsewhere, this is understandable because women have poorer health compared to men. Regarding the major occupations the old were engaged in, 18.5 per cent were doing their own farming, sometimes combined with agricultural labour elsewhere or business. Men comprised 23 per cent in this group while women only 14 per cent. Sixteen per cent were engaged in agricultural labour—men to the extent of 17.5 per cent and women 14.6 per cent. Thus there was not much difference between men and women in the percentage doing agricultural labour. On the whole, more than 34 per cent were engaged in agriculture. About 18 per cent of the women reported were doing household work. Looking after the cattle has traditionally been a task performed by old men. The age distribution of those not working is set out in Table 5.4.

Table 5.4
Elderly Villagers Not Working by Age Group

Age Group	Total Men	Men Not Working	Men Not Working (%)	Total Women	Women Not Working	Women Not Working (%)
60–64	60	13	21.0	108	31	28.7
65–69	81	23	28.4	97	42	43.3
70–74	68	35	51.5	53	32	60.4
75–79	36	20	55.6	28	25	89.3
80 and over	35	26	74.3	35	29	82.9
Total	280	117	41.8	321	159	49.5

The most striking point about the table is that the median age of the old men was 69 years while that of women was lower, i.e., 67 or thereabout. Surprisingly, women were younger on an average. Generally, all over the world women as a group live longer and are therefore older. Of course we are assuming that the ages were correctly reported.

Two additional points may be noted. First, in every age group, the percentage of women not working (even at household chores) was higher than men. Second, with increasing age, both men and women started working less and less as expected. As will be seen in the following section, rural men and women worked much more than their urban counterparts at the age of 50 or so.

Occupation at Age 50 or So

The old men and women were asked what occupation did they follow when they were near about 50 years old. Their answers are set out in Table 5.5.

Compared to Table 5.4, where almost 46 per cent of the old were not working, this table looks very different. At age 50 just

Table 5.5
Rural Old by Their Occupation at Age 50 or Thereabout

Occupation	Men	Women	Total	Per Cent
Own household work	1	26	27	4.5
Others' household work	0	2	2	0.3
Unskilled private service	14	4	18	3.0
Skilled private service	17	4	21	3.5
Own farming	135	162	297	49.4
Agricultural labour	74	107	181	30.1
Own business	20	9	29	4.8
Unskilled job in organized sector	9	1	10	1.7
Skilled job in organized sector	7	1	8	1.3
Not working	1	2	3	0.5
Begging	0	1	1	0.2
Looking after own cattle	1	1	2	0.3
Social work	1	1	2	0.3
Total	280	321	601	100.0

one man and two women were not working. About half the men and women worked on their own farms, sometimes combining this with agricultural labour, business or service. Men and women worked almost equally, women working perhaps more than men. Men had slightly more diversified occupations than women. Table 5.5 clearly brings out that agriculture was the mainstay of the rural old, who either did their own farming or were engaged in agricultural labour.

Reduction of Work in Old Age

The old villagers were asked to talk about the extent of work they did in old age. Could they work as much as they did at 50 or thereabout? Were they forced to reduce their work? Their wide-ranging replies are shown in Table 5.6.

Almost 14 per cent were in absolutely good health and did not feel the need to reduce their workload. The work of almost 72.7 per cent was affected due to bad health. These included the 35.6 per cent who had to stop work completely, about 9 per cent who had bad health but could not afford to rest due to responsibilities, and 28 per cent who had reduced work due to bad health.

Table 5.6
Reduction in Work With Aging

Reduction in Work	Men	Women	Total	Per Cent
No reduction, health quite good	46	37	83	13.8
Health not good but cannot afford to reduce the work	29	26	55	9.2
Reduced due to bad health	88	80	168	28.0
Work continued because it is light	3	4	7	1.2
Work stopped due to ill health	89	125	214	35.6
Work reduced because no responsibility	8	23	31	5.2
Had to stop compulsorily	4	0	4	0.7
Left work because it was heavy	13	26	39	6.5
Total	280	321	601	100.0

While the rural elderly might have reduced their work, many were still not in a position to retire. They stated their retirement status slightly differently from the inmates of OAHs, as revealed in Table 5.7.

Table 5.7
Retirement Status of the Elderly Villagers

Retirement	Men	Women	Total	Per Cent
Still working	70	81	151	25.1
Still working, had to earn	66	40	106	17.6
Had to retire in spite of good health	4	0	4	0.7
Physically fit and retired, but in search of job	0	1	1	0.2
Retired, but doing another job	24	12	36	6.0
Health not good, retired, but seeking other work	2	0	2	0.3
Retired due to bad health	84	133	217	36.1
Retired, no need to work again	30	54	84	14.0
Total	280	321	601	100.0

About 51 per cent had actually retired. They comprised the 14 per cent who had comfortably retired, in the sense they did not need to work, and 36 per cent who had to give up working on account of bad health. A good 43 per cent were still working; the rest had mostly retired but were wanting to work for various reasons. The aged villagers were asked whether they worked and if not, why. As Table 5.8 shows, a little less than half (first two categories) worked and wanted to continue working. Two per cent were physically handicapped and hence never worked. The most common reason for not working was bad health.

Table 5.8
Current Working Status of the Rural Old

Working Status	Men	Women	Total	Per Cent
Still working though old	51	54	105	17.5
Will continue to work as long as able to	106	77	183	30.4
Stopped working after 60	17	31	48	8.0
Never got work	1	2	3	0.5
Did not work, bad health	69	102	171	28.5
Never worked, handicapped	8	4	12	2.0
Did not work, no need	28	51	79	13.1
Total	280	321	601	100.0

Age at Retirement

The rural elderly were asked about the age of retirement and whether it should be changed, etc. The concept of a retirement age was not really known to them. In their understanding people retired when they suffered from bad health, which was a part of the aging process. In the agricultural sector there is no 'age of retirement'. Thus more than 81 per cent had no opinion on this matter as seen in Table 5.9. Half of the remaining i.e., 10 per cent, thought that retirement with aging has to be accepted. Three per cent wanted the age of retirement to be raised.

Another question which seemed rather strange for some was one regarding old-age pension. They were not aware that old-age pension schemes existed and that the elderly could be helped with some of their problems through money payments. Sixty-four per cent were happy to hear about old-age pensions and thought that the government should incur the expenditure. The remaining 36 per cent could not conceive of such pensions.

Table 5.9
Opinion of the Elderly Villagers on 'Age of Retirement'

Opinion	Men	Women	Total	Per Cent
No opinion, no concern	208	282	490	81.5
Retirement with age is OK	29	32	61	10.1
Age at retirement should be raised	15	3	18	3.0
Retirement resented because of responsibilities (dependency load and own needs)	23	3	26	4.3
Retirement resented because very fit	5	1	6	1.0
Total	280	321	601	100.0

Persons the Elderly Lived With

With whom were the old villagers living? The answers can be found in Table 5.10.

Table 5.10
With Whom Were the Rural Old Living

Persons Living With	Men	Women	Total	Per Cent
Alone	11	46	57	9.5
With spouse	48	31	79	13.1
With spouse, son, and his family	180	197	377	62.7
With grandchildren	3	4	7	1.2
With daughter unmarried or married	3	7	10	1.7
With daughter and son-in-law	3	11	14	2.3
With other relatives	9	13	22	3.7
With widowed daughter-in-law	1	5	6	1.0
I am the head of family, I don't live with anybody, others do	21	7	28	4.7
With unrelated people	1	0	1	0.2
Total	280	321	601	100.0

The most common type of living arrangement comprised old villagers staying with their spouse, son and his family. These constituted 62.7 per cent. Almost 10 per cent were living alone, women much more so than men. This is quite different from what one saw in Chapter 3, where a larger number of men were observed to be living alone. An interesting category, constituting 4.7 per cent, was of persons, mostly men, who reported that they did not live with anybody. That they were heads of households and others lived with them. A proud category, they seemed quite conscious of their headship of the household.

Dependency Load of the Elderly

Another area of interest was the responsibility of child rearing that the old shouldered. Thus all the daughters and sons below 18 living with them or children under 18 of the sons with one parent dead were counted as the responsibility of the old. Grown-up but handicapped children were also included among the load of dependents. The data are presented in Table 5.11.

Table 5.11
Dependency Load of the Elderly Villagers

Load Count	Men	Women	Total	Per Cent
No responsibility	206	282	488	81.2
1	39	25	64	10.6
2	19	10	29	4.8
3	10	2	12	2.0
4	4	2	6	1.0
5	2	–	2	0.3
Total	280	321	601	100.0

After age 60, one does not expect the old to have any familial responsibilities and 81 per cent of the rural old surveyed by us were free of these. However, it is significant that 19 per cent old still carried this burden, with over 3 per cent having three or more dependents. As against 74 per cent of the men, 88 per cent of the women had no responsibilities. Since wives were often younger than men, for the same age group men were likely to shoulder a greater dependency load. This is clear from Table 5.12 which shows the percentage of men and women in various age groups with no responsibilities.

Thus in the age group 60–64, only 48 per cent of the men as against 75 per cent of the women were not responsible for their

Table 5.12
Rural Old Having No Responsibilities by Age Group

Age Group	Men Having No Respon- sibility	Total Men	Per Cent of Men with No Respon- sibility	Women Having No Respon- sibility	Total Women	Per Cent of Women Having No Respon- sibility
60–64	29	60	48.3	81	108	75.0
65–69	59	81	72.8	89	97	91.7
70–74	57	68	83.8	51	53	96.2
75–79	28	36	77.8	26	28	92.9
80 and over	33	35	94.3	35	35	100.0
Total	206	280	73.6	282	321	87.9

children. But for both men and women, this responsibility rapidly decreased with age.

Another aspect with crucial implications for the old was the number of sons they had and the age of the youngest one. If there was no son, after the daughters got married there was nobody to take care of the old. Similarly if the couple had only one son, his age was a matter of great significance.

As can be observed from Table 5.13, 16.5 per cent had no son at all. There were 25.6 per cent who had just one son and their ages have been taken cognizance of in this table. Those that had no son had to depend on their daughters, and those with only one son were totally dependent on him when the daughters were married. There were four men whose youngest son was in the age group 2–9 years—they must have much younger wives. The one woman whose youngest son was in this age group either wrongly reported her age or she had the child much after the age of 50. There were 20 women whose youngest son was in the age group 10–18. These women must have continued to give birth to children till they reached their menopause.

What Was the Size of the Household in Which the Old Were Living?

As Table 5.14 shows, 11 per cent of the households were inhabited by only one elderly person. In another 12 per cent of the households,

Table 5.13
Age of the Youngest Son of the Elderly

Age Group of the Son	Men	Women	Total	Per Cent
No son at all	37	62	99	16.5
2–9	4	1	5	0.8
10–18	42	20	62	10.3
19 and over	197	238	435	72.4
Total	280	321	601	100.0

Table 5.14
Household Size of the Rural Old

No of Persons in the Household	Men	Women	Total	Per Cent
1	20	46	66	11.0
2	35	37	72	12.0
3	25	25	50	8.3
4	35	42	77	12.8
5	38	41	79	13.1
6	41	50	91	15.2
7	41	38	79	13.1
8	20	20	40	6.7
9	25	22	47	7.8
Total	280	321	601	100.0

there was just one other person beside the old living in the house. If this was the spouse, which was not unlikely, she or he could be on the way to becoming old, if not already old. In 56 per cent of the households, there were five or more persons including the elderly. It appears that the old had an adequate number of people at hand who could look after them, if necessary. But it was the 11 per cent with nobody to take care of them, who needed the assistance of the government or voluntary agencies. Without medical aid or old-age pension, they would be in trouble if they were to fall ill. As evident from the case-studies presented in Chapter 7, they were helped out by the villagers.

Were the Old Educated? Were they Literate?

It was the answers to this item of information which more or less
indicated what level of development the villagers had reached,
which questions could be asked of them, and what ideas they
might have about old-age problems. Generally it is assumed that
the greater the age the less the education among the older
people. In rural India where higher education is absent, this inverse
correlation between age and literacy is high. Data regarding the
education level of all the old is presented in Table 5.15 and then
the literacy level for each age group in Table 5.16. A massive 78
per cent had received no education at all. Among men 62 per cent
were illiterate and among women 92 per cent. Another 13.5 per
cent had studied up to the 4th standard. A total of 6 persons
among the 601 surveyed had received education beyond the matri-
culation or higher secondary level.

Table 5.15
Level of Education of the Elderly Villagers

Level of Education	Men	Men Per Cent	Women	Women Per Cent	Total	Per Cent
Illiterate	173	61.8	295	91.9	468	77.9
1st to 4th std.	61	21.8	20	6.2	81	13.5
5th to 7th std.	35	12.5	2	0.6	37	6.2
8th to 11th std.	8	2.9	1	0.3	9	1.5
12th to graduate	0	–	1	0.3	1	0.1
Postgraduate	0	–	1	0.3	1	0.1
Doctor	3	1.1	0	–	3	0.5
Other technical	0	–	1	0.3	1	0.1
Total	280	100.0	321	100.0	601	100.0

Thus not only was the level of education low, but illiteracy was
widespread, especially among females. Naturally we wondered
whether such a village community had any idea about the problems
of the old elsewhere? Did they even have an inkling about the kind
of care that is given to the elderly or at least aspired to? Could they
conceive of OAHs? Did they understand the notion of retirement?
Had they ever heard of old-age pensions?

Table 5.16
Illiteracy Among the Rural Old by Age Group

Age Group	Illiterate Men	Total in Age Group	Per Cent Illiterate	Illiterate Women	Total in Age Group	Per cent Illiterate
60–64	31	60	51.7	91	108	84.3
65–69	49	81	60.5	93	97	95.9
70–74	36	68	52.9	50	53	94.3
75–79	26	36	72.2	26	28	92.9
80+	31	35	88.6	35	35	100.0
Total	173	280	61.8	295	321	91.9

One of the investigators noted that she found it difficult to ask some of the questions in the questionnaire because the village community she was interviewing was totally unaware of the problems that the old in an urbanized society usually faced. The elderly in cities have to contend with very serious issues—poverty, shortage of housing, and the generation gap, which causes friction not only between two male generations but also between women. The conflict between the modern, newly educated women regarding an improved female status and their traditional elders is assuming serious proportions. It has created problems unheard of in society before. The case-studies presented later show the clash between the highly educated and non-educated, between computer and management professionals and non-working or kitchen-cloistered yet happily placed women of earlier times. The vast difference in education levels has widened the gap between generations and the two groups rarely agree unless wisdom prevails. Even the gulf between the rural- and urban-based has increased so much that dialogue between the two seems impossible. This rural–urban divide is going to threaten the social fabric of the future; unless properly handled, it is likely to exacerbate the criminalization of society.

Despite the low level of education among males shown earlier, illiteracy increased with age. In the case of females that trend is not as clear-cut, but still the younger among the elderly were less illiterate; that is, illiteracy is less in the 60–64 than in the 65–80 age group and is the greatest in the age group 80+. There were only 3 women among 321 who had been educated beyond the secondary level.

Housing Status of the Elderly

The housing status of the rural old was compared with that of the inmates of old-age homes. As shown in the previous chapter in Table 4.9, many did not have homes of their own. In sharp contrast to this, the rural old had their own homes in a large percentage of cases; those without no shelter were nil compared to 31 among the inmates of the OAHs. As against 5 per cent of the elderly villagers living in somebody else's house, the percentage among the inmates of OAHs was 13.5. Certainly the level of housing of the rural old was much better.

As shown in Table 5.17, 82 per cent of the old had their own homes. Surprisingly, 1.7 per cent reported that the house they lived in belonged to the son. For villagers to report it this way seemed strange since such distinctions are usually not made in rural areas.

Table 5.17
Housing Status of the Elderly Villagers

Kind of Housing	Men	Women	Total	Per Cent
Own rented room or rooms	1	5	6	1.0
Own rented house	4	6	10	1.7
Rented flat	0	1	1	0.2
Somebody's house	11	19	30	5.0
Own house	241	251	492	81.9
Own hut	18	22	40	6.7
Son's house	0	10	10	1.7
Relative's house	5	7	12	2.0
Total	280	321	601	100.0

Though the housing of the villagers looked better on paper compared to that of the inmates of the OAH one could easily guess the kind of housing they had. From the point of view of opening OAHs for them their expectations were modest. In fact the villagers were so used to inconveniences that their old hardly complained of shortage of housing, as they did in cities. But since the administration cannot afford to provide the elderly with any minimum standard of housing, the best way to help the old in villages is to offer them old-age pensions which can at least cover their present level of needs, which of course is very low.

Even at the low level of housing which the villagers had, the number of rooms available to them was significant. This is relevant considering the condition of the old. If they wanted to rest, could they do so behind some partition if not in the kitchen? Moreover if the elderly got bedridden, living in the same room as them is not a very comfortable experience for other family members even if accustomed to living in confined housing conditions. Hence, one expected houses to have at least two rooms. Were these available in the villages? The answers are given in Table 5.18.

Table 5.18
Number of Rooms in the Housing of Elderly Villagers

No. of Rooms	Men	Women	Total	Per Cent
One	85	108	193	32.1
Two	102	116	218	36.3
Three	46	49	95	15.8
Four	31	28	59	9.8
Five	9	11	20	3.3
Six	2	5	7	1.2
More than six	5	4	9	1.5
Total	280	321	601	100.0

When ill and/or old it is certainly not healthy to live in one room along with others, especially when this room is a kitchen. But 32 per cent of the old lived in one-room houses. A little more than one-third lived in two-room houses. The remaining one-third lived in three or more rooms. Thus if at all, only one-third of the old had adequate housing while two-thirds were living under difficult conditions.

What Kind of Property Did the Old Have?

The property and assets held by the elderly villagers are shown in Table 5.19.

Table 5.19
Property and Assets of the Rural Old

Type of Property	Men	Women	Total	Per Cent
Nothing, except the house	80	135	215	35.8
House and business shop	3	0	3	0.5
House and only plot of land	22	11	33	5.5
Only hut	7	13	20	3.3
House, poultry and cattle	11	10	21	3.5
House and farm	103	114	217	36.1
House, farm, cattle, poultry	51	28	79	13.1
House, farm, business	3	9	12	2.0
House and rickshaw	0	1	1	0.2
Total	280	321	601	100.0

About 36 per cent of the old had nothing except the house they were living in. This meant that they would need to sell their labour for wages, but there was no employment for them in old age. One could add 3.3 to this group because they too had nothing but the hut in which they lived. Similarly 5.5 per cent had a small plot of land beside the house. Thus a total of 45 per cent had only some shelter but nothing else to depend on. They had to depend on somebody in old age. If they had sons, they could support their elderly parents. Otherwise the old would be left helpless.

About 51 per cent had farms, so that if they kept tenants, the old could be maintained partially if not wholly.

Since many of the old had stopped working, as seen earlier, they were asked to report their income at age 50.

As shown in Table 5.20, 10 per cent had an yearly income of less than Rs. 500. They could not support themselves since, as seen in an earlier chapter Rs. 1,000 is the income necessary for feeding one adult. (We will assume that the number of people in each income group is centred at the mid-point.) Another 15 per cent were living below the poverty line. At least they could not support any dependent and could only partly support themselves. They had an income of Rs. 750 a year and hence could support themselves only for 9 months, assuming that Rs. 80 per month is needed for one's support. In the income group with mid-point 1,500, 25.3 per cent could be assumed to be capable of bearing a load of more than one and a half adults. The income group with mid-point 3,750

Table 5.20
Yearly Income of the Rural Old at Age 50 or Thereabout

Level of Income	Men	Women	Total	Per Cent
No Income	3	24	27	4.5
–500	12	23	35	5.8
501–1,000	33	57	90	15.0
1,001–2,000	69	83	152	25.3
2,001–5,500	76	89	165	27.5
5,501–10,500	39	15	54	9.0
10,501–15,500	10	4	14	2.3
15,501–20,500	10	0	10	1.7
20,500+	3	2	5	0.8
Not reported	25	24	49	8.2
Total	280	321	601	100.0

had 27.5 per cent old capable of supporting 2.9 adults. Thus the male adult in this income group could at the age of 50 support his wife and two children (equivalent to half an adult). Only 14 per cent had the capacity to earn more than that, and they could save only if they did not spend more than Rs. 80 per adult. In other words, it is clear why people did not have much savings. Of course, one has to remember that 51 per cent had some land, as seen earlier. So in their case if the dependents could work on the farm, the elderly, could make a living. Thus, these villagers could fall back on land if that gave them enough income, not on savings.

Savings of the Old

In Table 5.21 the savings of the old are set out. In fact, there was no cash saving, but the land was theirs which we have not taken into account. We do not have accurate data on the landholdings of the villagers.

Of the 601 elderly persons surveyed, 96.5 per cent had no savings at all. Four men had Rs. 9,000, 12,000, 15,000 and 25,000 respectively, and two women had Rs. 25,000 and 50,000 respectively. In other words, very few had any savings. When the old were asked whether they had saved for the present phase of their lives, many found the question strange. They said, considering that they

Table 5.21
Savings of the Elderly Villagers

Savings (Rs.)	Men	Women	Total	Per Cent
None	267	313	580	96.5
Upto 1,000	4	4	8	1.3
1,001–2,000	2	0	2	1.3
2,000–3,000	2	1	3	0.5
Above 3,000	5	3	8	1.3
Total	280	321	601	100.0

had not had enough even for their requirements in their younger days, how could they have saved for old age.

Reasons for not Being Able to Save For Old Age

As seen from Table 5.22, 35 per cent argued that they had not saved because their earnings had been just enough to take care of their needs in their productive years. Another 24 per cent said that they had not had enough even to meet these. Thus in the case of 59 per cent, there had been no possibility of savings. Five per cent explained that they had sons who could look after them and hence they had not felt the need to save for old age. An additional 26 per cent had thought that since they had land or some other asset, there was no need to save. Then there were a few cases who had land but no one to cultivate it. There were some whose savings had been looted. Others had used their savings for house construction or the marriage or education of their sons. Thus for a variety of reasons, few had been able to save.

With no savings, the old had to work even after they turned 60. The age at which they had retired is given in Table 5.23.

Forty-six per cent of the elderly villagers were still working. Among them 47 per cent were women and 53 per cent men. Seventeen per cent retired in the age group 50–59 with a median age of about 55. Similarly 27 per cent retired at the age of 65, and about 8 per cent after 70 years of age. This trend was as expected. Now one may note the ages of those that were working. These are shown in Table 5.24.

Table 5.22
Reasons of the Rural Old for not Saving

Reason for not Saving	Men	Women	Total	Per Cent
No need to save because sons were there	14	17	31	5.2
Earning insufficient	55	87	142	23.6
Earning just enough	97	116	213	35.4
Spendthrift habits	2	0	2	0.3
Savings were utilized somewhere else	2	10	12	2.0
Savings were looted	1	1	2	0.3
Utilized for son's marriage	11	13	24	4.0
There were some assets such as land, etc.	87	71	158	26.3
Have land though no one to cultivate	2	0	2	0.3
Savings spent in house construction	5	2	7	1.2
Spent in the education of the children	3	4	7	1.2
Not reported	1	0	1	0.2
Total	280	321	601	100.0

Table 5.23
Age of Retirement of the Rural Old

Age Group of Retirement	Men	Women	Total	Per Cent
Still working	145	129	274	45.6
Never worked	1	2	3	0.5
30–39	0	1	1	0.2
40–49	1	5	6	1.0
50–59	33	71	104	17.3
60–69	75	90	165	27.4
70–79	19	20	39	6.5
80 and over	6	3	9	1.5
Total	280	321	601	100.0

Table 5.24
Age Distribution of Elderly Villagers Still Working

Age Group	Working Men	Per Cent of Age Group	Working Women	Per Cent of Age Group	Total	Per Cent
60–64	44	73.3	60	55.6	104	38.0
65–69	53	65.4	47	48.5	100	36.5
70–74	25	36.8	19	35.8	44	16.1
75–79	15	41.7	1	3.6	16	5.8
80 and over	8	22.9	2	5.7	10	3.6
Total	145		129		274	100.0

It is worth noting that the percentage of those working clearly declines with age. The percentage of women working was not only lower than that of men but it also declined faster with age.

Reasons For Retirement

Since for a large majority of the rural old retirement is voluntary, the reasons why they had retired were of significant interest. Were they ill or too disabled to work? The answers to this question are analyzed in Table 5.25.

Table 5.25
Reasons for Retirement of the Rural Old

Reasons	Men	Women	Total	Per Cent
Not retired	145	129	274	45.6
Health bad	76	131	207	34.4
Heavy work	42	49	91	15.1
No need to work	2	6	8	1.3
Retired according to rules	12	4	16	2.7
Voluntary retirement	2	0	2	0.3
Disabled for work	1	2	3	0.5
Total	280	321	601	100.0

As seen from Table 5.25, a little less than half of those surveyed had not yet retired. The other half had retired mainly because of bad health or they found the work too taxing for their age. This was not unexpected in a community that had never been well-off and just about managed to subsist.

To conclude, in the absence of modernization, the villagers did not seem too worried about problems of old age. They often depended on their neighbours in times of need. With almost 100 per cent still fully occupied at about age 50 and 80 per cent engaged in agriculture, where there is no notion of 'age of retirement', old age did not present a very distinct phase for the elderly villagers. Poverty and want had marked their entire life. The only difference was that in old age their health had deteriorated. In contrast, a good 46 per cent of their urban counterparts had stopped working by age 50. However, a vast majority of them did not have a house of their own unlike the rural old, most of whom lived in their own homes, albeit inadequate by any reasonable standards. However, there is a need to provide old-age pensions to the helpless villagers—an inexpensive way of solving their problems of want.

6

Is the Offer of Old-Age Security Possible?

From the interviews of the old, both in the villages and old-age homes, it was clear that the problem of poverty was more serious than that of aging. In many OAHs the inmates were capable of working; even if they could not do heavy chores, they managed to do some light work. Thus, if they could be engaged in similar tasks outside, there would be no need for them to come to OAHs. Inadequacy of pensions was another reason why some of the pensioners had to go to OAHs. As for the villagers, though they were content with their situation, their standard of living was low. They were always short of money, with the constraints being felt much more keenly as they grew older. Moreover, as there was little medicated survival, entailing a lot of nursing, problems on that front were rare. The offer of old-age pensions even at a meagre level can solve their problems to a reasonable extent. The OAH is a costly answer in view of the very limited funds available and the villagers did not need it. Old-age pensions would be a much better solution to their problems.

In India where poverty is rampant and the condition of the old very unsatisfactory, many states have thought of giving old-age pensions. But apart from Kerala, very few reports on the subject exist. Even in the case of Maharashtra workers in the relevant government departments were unaware of the existence of an old-age pension scheme. The only information available was that it was sanctioned in 1979–80 and the amount of pension per person was to be Rs. 30 per month. But nothing regarding the size of operations seemed to be known. Though Rs. 30 a month seems a meagre amount, many of the old hardly had any cash and the sum could help them buy a number of things they needed. In fact, it seemed that the elderly villagers were usually able to get food from their helpers but ready cash was a serious problem.

Survey of Old-Age Pension Schemes in Various Regions of India

Some data on the subject are available from a study by Chanana and Talwar (1987), extracts from which have been reproduced below.

The elderly who have worked in organized sectors during their lives have been and still are covered by social insurance schemes such as pensions, gratuities, leave encashment and provident fund disbursements payable upon their retirement. Such systems have been in use since 1871. They cover approximately 11 per cent of the population, who are likely to be economically better off compared with those who have worked in the unorganized sector. The latter constitute around 89 per cent of the elderly population. Out of this, the vast majority of the elderly probably worked for low wages and thus had little or no savings to enable them to meet their old-age needs.

Old age pensions have been introduced by state governments mostly for the destitute and infirm. It is worthwhile noting the distribution of states and union territories in India by eligibility for pension criteria in Table 6.1.

Thus, old-age pension has been provided by state governments mostly for the destitute and infirm. In 1957 the Uttar Pradesh government became the first to introduce an old-age pension scheme. Since then similar schemes have been introduced by other state governments—they were in operation in 16 out of 22 major states prior to 1980. All states and union territories, except Arunachal Pradesh, currently have such schemes. The level of pension provided by the various regions is set out in Table 6.2.

Table 6.1
Distribution of States and Union Territories by Pension Eligibility Criteria

Eligibility Criteria	Number of States and Union Territories
The destitute, 65 years of age (relaxation of requirement for physically handicapped destitutes)	9
Persons 65 years of age, widows, and physically handicapped	6
The destitute, 60 years of age, and widows and the infirm of any age	4
Persons 60 years of age (relaxation of requirement for the physically handicapped)	4
Persons 90 years of age and invalids 60 years of age	1
The destitute: males, 65 years of age and females, 60 years of age	2
The destitute: 80 years of age	1
The destitute: males, 58 years of age and females, 55 years of age	1
All disabled	2
Total	30

Table 6.2
Distribution of States and Union Territories by Size of Old-Age Pension Per Month

Pension Per Month (Rs.)	Number of States and Union Territories
30	4
35	1
40	2
45	1
50	5
60	17
Total	30

More detailed data would be very useful. What is especially worth examining are the schemes on paper and those actually implemented. In this chapter there is an attempt to do that for the state of Maharashtra.

Maharashtra falls in the category of those states paying Rs. 60 per month. From 1988 April it started giving Rs. 100 a month, as will be seen later in this chapter.

Generally the pension scheme covers only a small section of the elderly population. During the year 1984–85 only 3.7 million people were covered by the schemes in India, which accounted for about 7 per cent of the total elderly population in the country (Chanana and Talwar, 1987).

Details of the old-age pension schemes in various states of the country by 1991 are provided in Table 6.3 as given by Dr. Chandra Dave (1992). There is however a need for evaluating the implementation of all these schemes.

Social security is an essential programme which must be launched and continued. Not only are the aged a disproportionately low-income group but their ability to improve their own financial situation is very restricted. Personal savings, especially for the poor, are a difficult, risky and uncertain method of providing for retirement. Those who get private pension (a very negligible number) find the amount very inadequate. Barriers to employment of older persons further contribute to the need for social security. Rather than further discuss old-age security and its details we need to ask how, with minimal funds, the neediest among the poor can be served by a pension scheme. Thus for instance one will need to estimate how much money would be required in Maharashtra in order to give men and women above specific ages a pension. One will also have to estimate what percentage of the relevant category of population is served by schemes in the state such as Sanjay Niradhar Anudan Yojana (SNAY) discussed below.

The first pension scheme of 1979 did not take off in Maharashtra. However on 2 October 1980 a scheme called Sanjay Gandhi Niradhar Anudan Yojana was introduced. According to its rules financial assistance will be given at a uniform rate of Rs. 60 per month per person subject to a maximum of Rs. 150 per family if there are more than two destitute or physically handicapped persons in a family.

Under the scheme the following four broad categories of destitute and physically handicapped persons qualify for assistance:

(*a*) Old and infirm persons, above the age of 60 years in the case of women and 65 years in the case of men, who have

Table 6.3

Old-Age Pension Rate, Eligibility, Coverage, Expenditure and Provision by the Finance Commission

Sr. No.	Name of State/ UT	Current Rate of Pension (Rs. p.m.)	Minimum Age for Eligibility (in Years)	Total Population in 1981 (in '000s)	Number in 1981 of Persons of Age of 60+ (in '000s)	Number of Beneficiaries in 1987-88 (in '000s)	Per Cent Covered on 1981 Basis	Expenditure in 1987-88 (Rs. in Lakhs)	No. of Elderly Covered by FC Formula (in '000s)	Funds Provided Under FC Formula (Rs. in Lakhs)
1	2	3	4	5	6	7	8	9	10	11
	States									
1	Andhra Pradesh	30	65	53,550	3,559	817	23.0	2467.00	101.1	1285.20
2	Arunachal Pradesh	60	60	632	30	(227)*	0.8	2.00	1.3	15.17
3	Assam	60	65 males 60 females	19,897	1,293	33	2.6	235.22	39.8	477.53
4	Bihar	30	60	69,915	4,756	1,500	31.5	5013.45	139.8	1677.96
5	Goa (Daman and Diu)	60/50	60	1,087	74	55	74.3	26.98	2.2	26.09
6	Gujarat	60	60	34,086	2,029	44	2.2	331.16	68.2	818.06
7	Haryana	100	65	12,923	819	673	82.2	3336.32	25.8	310.15
8	Himachal Pradesh	60	65	4,281	321	57	17.8	384.83	8.6	102.74
9	Jammu and Kashmir	60	55	5,987	344	5	1.5	45.00	12.0	143.69
10	Karnataka	50	65 males 60 females	37,136	2,459	554	22.5	3057.45	74.3	891.26
11	Kerala	55/60	65	25,454	1,910	459	24.0	2901.51	50.9	610.90
12	Madhya Pradesh	100	60	52,179	3,364	163	4.8	1120.00	104.4	1252.30

13	Maharashtra	100	65 males 60 females	62,784	4,009	279	7.0	2107.00	125.6	1506.82
14	Manipur	60	65 males 60 females	1,421	83	11	13.3	11.00	2.8	34.10
15	Meghalaya	60	65 males 60 females	1,336	59	1	1.7	0.09	2.7	32.06
16	Mizoram	60	65 males 60 females	494	23	2	8.7	13.87	1.9	
17	Nagaland	100	70	775	46	2	4.3	17.82	1.6	18.60
18	Orissa	40	65	26,370	1,685	126	7.5	556.02	52.7	632.88
19	Punjab	100	65 males 60 females	16,789	1,309	90	6.9	492.93	33.6	402.94
20	Rajasthan	60	58 males 55 females	34,262	2,065	85	4.1	47.00	68.5	822.29
21	Sikkim	60	74 males 65 females	316	14	(101)*	0.7	3.96	0.6	7.58
22	Tamil Nadu	50	65	48,408	3,104	373	12.0	1584.36	96.8	1161.79
23	Tripura	75	70	2,053	145	22	15.2	194.01	4.1	49.27
24	Uttar Pradesh	100	65	1,10,862	7,682	129	1.7	861.34	221.7	2660.69
25	West Bengal	60	60	54,581	3,029	31	1.0	220.42	109.2	1309.94
	Total			6,77,578	44,211	5511	14.9	25030.74	1350.2	16250.01
	Union Territories									
26	A and N Islands	60	60	189	5	(115)*	2.3	1.00	–	–
27	Chandigarh	60	60 males 60 females	452	18	(70)*	0.9	1.31	–	–
28	D and N Haveli	60	65 males 60 females	104	4	(227)*	5.7	1.63	–	–

Table 6.3 (Continued)

Sr. No.	Name of State/ UT	Current Rate of Pension (Rs. p.m.)	Minimum Age for Eligibility (in Years)	Total Population in 1981 (in '000s)	Number in 1981 of Persons of Age of 60+ (in '000s)	Number of Beneficiaries in 1987–88 (in '000s)	Per Cent Covered on 1981 Basis	Expenditure in 1987–88 (Rs. in Lakhs)	No. of Elderly Covered by FC Formula (in '000s)	Funds Provided Under FC Formula (Rs. in Lakhs)
1	2	3	4	5	6	7	8	9	10	11
29	Delhi	100	60	6,220	279	3	1.1	22.00	–	–
30	Lakshadweep	100	60	40	2	(293)*	14.6	2.11	–	–
31	Pondicherry	60/100	60/75	604	41	2	4.9	9.8	–	–
	Total			7,609	349	5	1.7	37.85	–	–
	Total (States and UTs)			6,85,187	44,560	5516	4.5	25068.59	1350.2	16250.01

*: Negligible figures.

FC: Finance Commission.

Notes: Andhra Pradesh: The figures, which include those pertaining to the scheme of Pensions to Landless Agricultural Workers, are as reported on 5 August 1988 without indication of year.

Goa: Figures include those of the scheme of individual subsidy being implemented by Poovidoria (an autonomous organization in Goa).

Jammu and Kashmir: Figures relate to the year 1983–84.

Kerala: Figures relate to the year 1983–84.

Tripura: The state has four different old-age pension schemes; the figures are the totals of the four schemes.

West Bengal: Figures are exclusive of the beneficiaries under the Pension Scheme for Marginal Farmers.

Source: Dave (1992).

been incapacitated on account of age and infirmity and are
therefore unable to earn their own living.

(b) Persons who have been incapacitated and therefore unable
to earn their own living on account of any physical disability
like total blindness or any other severe physical or mental
disability like paraplegia or cerebral palsy or any long lasting
disease like leprosy, T.B. and cancer.

(c) Widows who are financially without support and are unable
to bring up their children below the age of 10 years.

(d) Children below 16 years of age in the case of boys and 18
years in the case of girls and dependents on and living with
the categories of persons mentioned under (a), (b) and (c)
above.

The government resolution, no. OAP-25594 dated the 15th June
1979, about the scheme also mentions that the old age pension
scheme should be withdrawn and the provision of Rs. 11 lakhs
made for the scheme for the current financial year should be
surrendered. All those persons who have already been sanctioned
pensions will be brought under the purview of the new scheme.

It was estimated by the government that about 1 lakh beneficiaries[1]
falling in the above-mentioned categories would be covered by the
new scheme. On this basis and at the rate of Rs. 60 per month per
person, the total expenditure incurred in a year would be Rs. 7.20
crores.

The application for financial assistance had to be submitted to
the talathi or gram sevak/assistant gram sevak or the tahsildar of
the area in which the applicant is residing. The application had to
be accompanied by a number of certificates: age certificate; dis-
ability/disease certificate; income and property certificate; destitution certificate; certificate regarding non-begging or mendicancy;
certificate regarding not being an inmate of any government or

---

[1] It is difficult to know how this estimate of 1 lakh was arrived at by the
government. This includes the physically and mentally incapacitated persons,
widows with small children, and the dependents of incapacitated persons. Our
interest was only in the old who deserved help according to the scheme. Besides, as
can be seen later in the chapter, this estimate of 1 lakh is too low and improperly
estimated. The basis of this estimate has not been explained. Moreover, even if the
estimate is correct, how could the expenditure for 1985–86 in Table 6.4 increase to
21 crores?

non-government or charitable institution or home; certificate of residency.

A committee of 5 non-official members, including a chairman, was appointed by the government. The tahsildar of each taluka was to be the secretary of this committee.

Disbursement of financial assistance to a beneficiary was to be made by the tahsildar every month. However, the beneficiary had to intimate the tahsildar that he was alive and there was no possibility of any change in his conditions. If the beneficiary were to migrate to another state, the assistance was to be discontinued.

All payments of financial assistance were to be made to the applicants by money orders, such money-orders being issued on the 26th of each month, so that the beneficiary receives the money-order before 3rd of the following month. The cost on account of money-order charges was to be borne by government and was to be met from financial allotments placed at the disposal of the tahsildar. It was the responsibility of the Director of Social Welfare to place the necessary allotment of funds at the disposal of the collectors based on the requirements of the tahsildars. Collectors were responsible for ensuring proper expenditure out of the allotment, maintenance of accounts, internal auditing of such accounts, etc. The collector in this connection was to forward a quarterly report to the Director of Social Welfare and government in the Social Welfare Department.

It was the responsibility of the tahsildar to process all applications within a period of two weeks at the maximum. There was right of appeal to the state level committee against the decision taken by the taluka level committee. The verdict of the state level committee was supposed to be final.

If the beneficiary died, the village officer in the case of the gram panchayat area or the municipal authority in the case of municipal area were supposed to report the fact to the tahsildar immediately after the death occurred so that there was stoppage of the assistance forthwith.

Grant of financial assistance was supposed to be a matter of absolute discretion of the government and could be refused or stopped with or without giving any reasons by the sanctioning authority. The decision of the sanctioning authority could not be questioned in any court of law.

The government resolution with regard to the above is presented in Appendix 6.1 to this chapter. According to the application form for this scheme, to be a *niradhar* (a helpless person), one should neither have sons, aged 18 and above, nor a spouse. Thus, a person could be categorized as *niradhar* only if these 'close' relatives did not exist. In other words, daughters or their relatives were not counted while considering the extent of helplessness.

This scheme remained unchanged till 1991 except for the fact that the financial assistance was increased to Rs. 100 per month per person from April 1988.

In what follows we examine the Sanjay Niradhar Anudan Yojana (SNAY) for the nine years 1981 to 1990. The total expenditure on SNAY during this period is presented in Table 6.4. Beside the actual expenditure for each year (column 2) ending in February, the total number of beneficiaries is also given. One needs to check the consistency of the data. The expenditure continuously increased till 1988 except during 1983–84. In April 1988 the sum paid to the beneficiary was increased from Rs. 720 a year per person to Rs. 1,200—a big rise in the expenditure. If there were no other expenses, the total number of beneficiaries multiplied by Rs. 720 should give the expected expenditure per annum (column 4). Column 6 shows that the actual expenditure was 10 per cent higher than expected in 1981–82, 13 per cent lower in 1982–83, 28 per cent lower in 1983–84, 24 per cent higher in 1984–85, etc. It should be possible for the administration to broadly explain these variations. The same method of checking the consistency of the data is possible from column 5, which should show the figure of 720 for all the years between 1981 and 1988 and the figure 1,200 for the last two years.

Be that as it may, the data bring out one fact that SNAY had a provision of Rs. 376 million in 1989–90 which could be distributed to people under various pretexts and this was a sizable amount. It is only for the two years 1983 to 1985 where the data seem erroneous. No wonder that in 1985 suspecting corruption, government closely scrutinized the programme and weeded out fraudulent elements. Moreover the explanation for the deviations in columns 5 and 6 could be that when more than two persons in one family were eligible for the benefit, they could not get more than the equivalent of 2.5 units of benefit.

The beneficiaries mentioned in Table 6.4 include all the four categories (*a*), (*b*), (*c*) and (*d*) listed in the government resolution. Our interest in the present chapter is restricted to only elderly, covered by category (*a*). The data on beneficiaries for various years do not classify them as (*a*), (*b*), (*c*) and (*d*) except for the year 1989–90. Fortunately, for this year a categorywise break-up of the data on beneficiaries is available for each of the 30 districts of the state of Maharashtra and are presented in Table 6.5. However, we have no means to check the figures in the various columns.

Table 6.4
Checking the Consistency of the Data on Expenditure and Beneficiaries of SNAY

Year	Actual Expenditure Rs.	Total Beneficiaries	Expected Expenditure (3) X Annual Benefit Rs.	(2)/(3)	(2)/(4)
(1)	*(2)*	*(3)*	*(4)*	*(5)*	*(6)*
1981–82	130,500,000	165,120	118,886,400	790.33	1.10
1982–83	184,000,000	293,818	211,548,960	626.24	0.87
1983–84	137,400,000	265,721	191,319,120	517.08	0.72
1984–85	187,200,000	210,191	151,337,520	890.62	1.24
1985–86	189,700,000	295,149	212,507,280	642.73	0.89
1986–87	205,300,000	273,486	196,909,920	750.68	1.04
1987–88	210,700,000	278,762	200,708,640	755.84	1.05
1988–89	321,624,400	295,815	354,978,000	1087.25	0.91
1989–90	376,313,640	321,576	385,891,200	1170.22	0.98

Note: Annual benefit was Rs. 720 till 1987–88 and Rs. 1,200 subsequently.

Using the 1991 census figures, the percentage of beneficiaries to total population may be calculated (column 9). For Maharashtra as a whole, beneficiaries formed 0.45 per cent of the total population. In operation for over 10 years, SNAY could be considered mature and known to people. However, variations in the last column are very large and difficult to explain. One can only note that the percentages are generally low for western Maharashtra and much higher for the Vidarbha and Marathvada regions. In other words the percentage was about 0.36 in western Maharashtra, 0.74 in Marathvada, and 0.64 in Vidarbha. The percentages were exceptionally low for Bombay and Thane, which is understandable as these two districts are the most industrialized—with industrial-ization not only do most of the employables get employed, but the disabled tend to migrate out to escape the higher cost of living. The Marathvada and Vidarbha regions are slightly backward com-pared to the western Maharashtra region, but does that explain the fact that the number of beneficiaries there were twice or more than those in western Maharashtra? There seem to be two possible expla-nations for this observation. First, these backward regions did have a larger percentage of those deserving payment under the SNAY. The other possibility is that these regions employed different definitions of those 'deserving' payments. Not being mutually exclusive, both possibilities are likely to exist and, closer examination is necessary to understand the observed differences.

The data on beneficiaries were looked at from another angle. The total beneficiaries for the year 1989–90 were classified as old and others. In Table 6.6 the male beneficiaries above 65 and female beneficiaries above 60 are expressed as percentages of the total number of beneficiaries. It is worth noting that two-thirds of all beneficiaries were elderly males and females. Here the differ-ences in the three sub-regions are not so great. Western Maharashtra had 67 per cent of old beneficiaries, Marathvada had 69 per cent, and Vidarbha 71 per cent. Thus, one can safely say that of the total beneficiaries, two-thirds were getting old-age pensions through SNAY.

Another observation from Table 6.6 is that the percentage of elderly female beneficiaries (48 per cent) is more than twice that of male beneficiaries (20 per cent). The reasons for this large difference are several: First, females were eligible for the pension after the age of 60 as against 65 in the case of males. Second, women live longer on an average than men, especially once they have crossed the child-bearing ages. Third, many more were widowed and helpless than men. Fourth, their health was worse compared to that of men.

Thus, while the data on the whole seemed consistent, problems arose when they were further analyzed.

Table 6.7 gives estimates of the expected number of elderly beneficiaries under certain assumptions. First, the numbers of men above 65 and women above 60 are estimated and then the necessary multipliers are applied to them. The following four assumptions are made in the estimation: (*i*) the male population of 1991 had

Table 6.5
The Beneficiaries of SNAY in 1989–90 Under Various Heads and Percentage Beneficiaries to Total Population in Districts

District (1)	Males 65+ (2)	Females 60+ (3)	Widows (4)	Dependent Children (5)	Disabled (6)	Total Beneficiaries (7)	Total Population M+F (8)	Percentage of Beneficiaries to Total Population (9)
			Western Maharashtra					
Bombay	412	2,200	1,759	–	636	5,007	9908547	0.05
Thane	1,195	3,783	1,127	1,716	1,456	9,277	5224679	0.18
Raigad	1,196	4,092	1,600	3,243	729	10,860	1818130	0.60
Ratnagiri	1,050	5,092	1,379	–	498	8,019	1539416	0.52
Sindhudurg	375	3,218	635	–	484	4,712	830726	0.57
Nasik	1,135	4,060	709	–	814	6,718	3837596	0.18
Ahmednagar	2,637	7,518	1,831	–	1,301	13,287	3362359	0.40
Dhule	1,295	4,379	769	–	470	6,913	2529346	0.27
Jalgaon	3,197	8,552	1,783	3,587	990	18,109	3184688	0.57
Pune	1,536	6,922	2,119	4,554	1,634	16,765	5494336	0.31
Solapur	4,183	8,193	1,478	2,624	1,533	18,011	3224034	0.56
Satara	1,239	4,087	913	–	999	7,238	2444857	0.30
Sangli	1,210	3,184	658	–	643	5,695	2197977	0.26
Kolhapur	1,120	5,136	2,547	–	1,303	10,106	2979352	0.34

District							
Marathwada							
Aurangabad	1,981	7,260	2,556	3,663	1,265	16,725	2209052	0.76
Parbhani	4,757	8,540	2,617	—	1,384	17,298	2113168	0.82
Nanded	3,773	9,367	5,035	—	2,577	20,752	2314783	0.90
Osmanabad	1,625	3,792	1,026	1,666	1,483	9,592	1271840	0.75
Latur	5,300	6,361	1,828	—	1,488	14,977	1672477	0.90
Beed	2,708	4,858	1,647	—	886	10,099	1818499	0.56
Jalna	1,384	4,448	1,064	—	—	6,896	1364718	0.51
Vidarbha							
Amravati	3,664	7,032	7,485	—	782	18,963	2206562	0.86
Akola	6,522	11,563	3,065	—	1,110	22,260	2211016	1.01
Yavatmal	4,871	8,728	1,800	—	1,525	16,924	2073708	0.82
Buldhana	3,101	5,989	1,995	—	978	12,063	1881438	0.64
Nagpur	3,809	7,987	3,757	—	2,071	17,624	3274974	0.54
Wardha	2,115	3,532	1,353	—	653	7,653	1065589	0.72
Chandrapur	1,528	2,835	1,107	—	603	6,073	1768945	0.34
Gadchiroli	431	1,331	806	—	543	3,111	785626	0.40
Bhandara	2,391	4,671	1,948	—	341	9,351	2103276	0.44
Total	71,740	168,710	58,396	21,053	31,179	351,078	78711714	0.45

Table 6.6
Male Beneficiaries Above 65 and Female Beneficiaries Above 60 Who Benefited by SNAY

District	Actual Benefi- ciaries 65+ Years Males	Actual Benefi- ciaries 65+ Years Females	Total* Benefi- ciaries	Percent- age of 65+ Male Benefi- ciaries	Percent- age of 60+ Female Benefi- ciaries	Percent- age of Old Benefi- ciaries (Males and Females)
Western Maharashtra						
Bombay	412	2,200	5,007	8.23	43.94	52.17
Thane	1,195	3,783	9,277	12.88	40.78	53.66
Raigad	1,196	4,092	10,860	11.01	37.68	48.69
Ratnagiri	1,050	5,092	8,019	13.09	63.50	76.59
Sindhudurg	375	3,218	4,712	7.96	68.29	76.25
Nasik	1,135	4,060	6,718	16.89	60.43	77.33
Ahmednagar	2,637	7,518	13,287	19.85	56.58	76.43
Dhule	1,295	4,379	6,913	18.73	63.34	82.08
Jalgaon	3,197	8,552	18,109	17.65	47.23	64.88
Pune	1,536	6,922	16,765	9.16	41.29	50.45
Solapur	4,183	8,193	18,011	23.22	45.49	68.71
Satara	1,239	4,087	7,238	17.12	56.47	73.58
Sangli	1,210	3,184	5,695	21.25	55.91	77.16
Kolhapur	1,120	5,136	10,106	11.08	50.82	61.90
Marathvada						
Aurangabad	1,981	7,260	16,725	11.84	43.41	50.47
Parbhani	4,757	8,540	17,298	27.50	49.37	76.87
Nanded	3,773	9,367	20,752	18.18	45.14	63.32
Osmanabad	1,625	3,792	9,592	16.94	39.53	56.47
Latur	5,300	6,361	14,977	35.39	42.47	77.86
Beed	2,708	4,858	10,099	26.81	48.10	74.92
Jalna	1,384	4,448	6,896	20.07	64.50	84.57
Vidarbha						
Amravati	3,664	7,032	18,963	19.32	37.08	56.40
Akola	6,522	11,563	22,260	29.30	51.95	81.24
Yavatmal	4,871	8,728	16,924	28.78	51.57	80.35
Buldhana	3,101	5,989	12,063	25.71	49.65	75.35
Nagpur	3,809	7,987	17,624	21.61	45.32	66.93
Wardha	2,115	3,532	7,653	27.63	46.15	73.76
Chandrapur	1,528	2,835	6,073	25.16	46.68	72.01
Gadchiroli	431	1,331	3,111	13.85	42.78	56.64
Bhandara	2,391	4,671	9,351	25.57	49.95	75.28
Total	71,740	168,710	351,078	20.43	48.05	68.26

* Total beneficiaries include all besides the elderly who benefit by the scheme.

Table 6.7
**Expected and Actual Number of Elderly Male and Female Beneficiaries
Coming Under SNAY in Various Districts**

District	Expected Beneficiaries		Actual Beneficiaries		Actual as % of Expected	
	Males 65+	Females 60+	Males 65+	Females 60+	Males 65+	Females 60+
(1)	(2)	(3)	(4)	(5)	(6)	(7)
Western Maharashtra						
Bombay	11027.62	15976.86	412	2200	3.74	13.77
Thane	5628.75	8753.28	1195	3783	21.23	43.22
Raigad	1830.34	3273.05	1196	4092	65.34	125.02
Ratnagiri	1409.67	3018.96	1050	5092	74.49	168.67
Sindhudurg	786.20	1584.07	375	3218	47.70	203.15
Nasik	3986.98	6690.01	1135	4060	28.47	60.69
Ahmednagar	3487.77	5871.21	2637	7518	75.61	128.05
Dhule	2614.24	4433.34	1295	4379	49.54	98.77
Jalgaon	3321.12	5529.76	3197	8552	96.26	154.65
Pune	5744.12	9514.69	1536	6922	26.74	72.75
Solapur	3371.48	5581.60	4183	8193	124.07	146.79
Satara	2432.59	4452.02	1239	4087	50.93	91.80
Sangli	2263.70	3866.76	1210	3184	53.45	82.34
Kolhapur	3073.96	5231.63	1120	5136	36.44	98.17
Marathvada						
Aurangabad	2322.45	3802.54	1181	7260	50.85	190.93
Parbhani	2189.04	3695.13	4757	8540	217.31	231.12
Nanded	2408.17	4029.52	3773	9367	156.67	232.46
Osmanabad	1325.77	2209.36	1625	3792	122.57	171.63
Latur	1741.91	2907.94	5300	6361	304.26	218.75
Beed	1891.01	3167.11	2708	4858	143.20	153.39
Jalna	1411.13	2390.95	1384	4448	98.08	186.03
Vidarbha						
Amravati	2306.18	3822.39	3664	7032	158.88	183.97
Akola	2307.97	3835.18	6522	11563	282.59	301.50
Yavatmal	2154.50	3614.94	4871	8728	226.08	241.44
Buldhana	1948.87	3290.13	3101	5989	159.12	182.03
Nagpur	3448.87	5627.15	3809	7987	110.44	141.94
Wardha	1111.56	1849.68	2115	3532	190.27	190.95
Chandrapur	1838.41	3082.70	1538	2835	83.66	91.96
Gadchiroli	804.95	1389.47	431	1331	53.54	95.79
Bhandara	2141.22	3744.25	2391	4671	111.67	124.75
Total	82330.55	136235.68	70950	168710	86.18	123.84

4.05 per cent men above 65 years of age; (*ii*) the 1991 female population had 7.16 per cent women above 60 years of age; (*iii*) 50 per cent of the total men and women were living below the poverty line in the age groups relevant here; (*iv*) and 10 per cent of those living below the poverty line were helpless in the sense that they had no son, spouse or grandson who could work and look after them.

These assumptions do not look unrealistic. The past percentages of the old in the relevant ages are projected for 1991. Generally 40 per cent of the population in the country live below the poverty line. Their percentage among the old may reasonably be assumed to be 50. The fourth assumption of 10 per cent living alone is based on the findings of this study (especially Chapter 3 and 5). Table 6.7 also shows the actual number of elderly beneficiaries. When expressed as percentages of the expected number of beneficiaries, they should have worked out to 100. Instead, one got quite a range of varying figures. For the state as a whole, the actual number of male beneficiaries as a percentage of the expected number comes to 86 which is not unreasonably deviant. The corresponding figure for women is higher (124) but again not inconceivable. One may however note that from among those eligible, more women than men have been favoured, justifiably or unjustifiably. In other words, if there was corruption in the allocation of pension, it worked in favour of women on the whole.

The districtwise deviations from hundred are, except in a few cases, difficult to explain. The Bombay and Thane observations are understandable because these cities may have fewer elderly persons than the average for the state as a whole. Similarly the Raigad, Ratnagiri and Sindhudurg observations are not surprising for exactly the opposite reasons—the migration of young adults from these districts to Bombay and Thane.

The remaining deviations, however, are not so easily understood. For instance, among the males above 65, the percentage of actual beneficiaries was 60 for western Maharashtra's 9 districts, 156 for the Marathvada districts, and 153 for the Vidarbha districts. For females above 60, the percentage of actual beneficiaries was 104 for western Maharashtra, 198 for Marathvada, and 173 for Vidarbha. These variations may be partly explained by (*i*) real differences and partly by (*ii*) irregularities, including corruption. Only the administration can throw light on the latter.

Further analysis was also constrained by the limited nature of the data. Districtwise data was available only for the year 1989–90.

On the other hand, the data for 14 tahsils of Pune district were available for 10 years. But a tahsilwise analysis also showed inexplicable variations. Could it be that the eligible did differ vastly from one tahsil to another? It would be worth investigating these differences more thoroughly. A sample of districts from the three regions can be taken and the pensioners interviewed. It is relatively easier now to contact the pensioners due to the change in the method of paying pensions. Previously, the pensions used to be sent by money-order at government cost which was not included in the expenditure on this scheme. But at present the pensions are paid through the bank so that the expenses on money-orders can be saved. The possibilities for conducting such a survey are worth exploring.

Every six months the elderly have to send a certificate to the government to indicate that they are alive. Other data such as applications by pensioners, deaths among them, etc., are also available. Though presently unutilized, if attempts are made to systematically gather and analyze such data, they could enrich the database on the elderly in the country.

As for old-age security in the organized sector, there are schemes providing pensions or provident funds which seem reasonable by Indian standards of living. But as is well-known, workers in the organized sector comprise less than 12 per cent or so.

For those that have some savings there are insurance schemes pertinent to old age such as Jeevan Akshay or Jeevan Dhara. Jeevan Akshay can be availed by those who are 50 years of age and above. It requires a lump sum investment. Monthly payment for life to the insured person works out to about 12.7 per cent of the investment, which is commensurate with income from other investment ventures. It offers an option to the policy-holder of taking out 30 per cent of the principal after seven years of investment for a small reduction in the monthly income. In addition, the Jeevan Akshay policy entitles one to a tax rebate.

The main feature of the Jeevan Dhara policy is the facility of payment of premium over a period. The plan provides for a maximum deferment period of 35 years. The annuity payments start at the end of the deferment period. There are also schemes of the Unit Trust of India, such as Deferred Income Unit Scheme (DIUS 1990), which help the old.

Those whose annual income is less than Rs. 100,000 after the age of 65, get a 40 per cent reduction in payable tax under the income tax laws. But this concession covers only a small percentage of the population.

To conclude, the SNAY pension scheme in the state of Maharashtra is a very welcome one. It is helping the old and the destitute of the expected order. With an expenditure of Rs. 376 million in 1989–90, it has a substantial budget. What is lacking is the proper maintenance of payment records. In the case of government spending, one expects meticulous documentation of the expenses incurred. It is surprising to find such a state of affairs when actual payments of the order of crores of rupees are involved. Some contend that the data of the social welfare department always suffer from this deficiency. If it were improved, one may welcome the Maharashtra scheme of old-age pensions as a model for other states.

Appendix

Sanjay Gandhi Niradhar Anudan Yojana

Rules for Grant of Financial Assistance to Destitute And Physically Handicapped Persons

Preamble—Approximately, more than 48 per cent of the population in our country is living below the poverty line. Similarly, nearly 14 per cent of the population in the country is reported to be under severe destitution. Some measure of social security, howsoever small or insignificant it may appear to be, is therefore imperative. Persons who need immediate support are persons who have been incapacitated either due to old age or due to any severe physical disability or incurable disease and in such circumstances, have also nobody to support them. There are also widows, who being supportless, have also to look after and bring up small children below 10 years of age. They also need some financial support. Destitute, neglected, victimised or deserted children or youthful offenders below the age of 16 years in the case of boys and 18 years in the case of girls are categories of persons whose maintenance, etc. is provided for in various Government institutions either within the provisions of the Bombay Children Act,

1948, or outside such provisions, that is, under non-statutory social welfare measure of Government or voluntary organizations. Such children therefore do not need any particular separate treatment under this programme. Similarly, beggars and mendicants come within the purview of the provisions of the Prevention of Begging Act, 1959, and, as such, cannot be considered under this social security programme.

2. Having regard to these paramount considerations Government has now decided to undertake a social security programme for providing financial support to the categories of persons mentioned above under the Sanjay Gandhi Niradhar Anudan Yojana as per the following rules:

1. *Title*—(i) These Rules may be called 'SANJAY GANDHI NIRADHAR ANUDAN YOJANA RULES, 1980'.

(*ii*) These Rules shall be applicable throughout the Maharashtra State and come into force with effect from 2nd October 1980.

2. *Categories of eligible persons*—The following categories of persons, having been residents of Maharashtra State for a period of not less than 15 years, shall be deemed to be eligible for grant of financial assistance under these Rules:

(*a*) Old and infirm persons, above the age of 60 years in case of women and 65 years in case of men who have been incapacitated on account of age and infirmity and are therefore unable to earn their own living.

(*b*) Persons who have been incapacitated and therefore unable to earn their own living on account of any physical disability like total blindness or any other severe physical or mental disability like paraplegia and cerebral palsy or any long duration disease like leprosy, T.B. and cancer.

(*c*) Widows who are financially supportless and are unable to bring up their small children below the age of 10 years.

(*d*) Children below 16 years of age in the case of boys and 18 years in the case of girls and dependent on and living with the categories of persons mentioned under (a), (b) and (c) above.

3. *Eligibility conditions* —Persons in the four broad categories mentioned in the foregoing rule shall be entitled to grant of financial assistance under these Rules if they satisfy the following conditions.

(*i*) He/She is not an inmate of any institution or home run by Government, voluntary organization, charitable organization or a local authority.

(*ii*) He/She is not following the profession of begging or is not a mendicant.

(*iii*) He/She is the resident of Maharashtra State for not less than 15 years.

(*iv*) He/She has no relative of 18 years of age and above, of the following categories, to financially support:- a son, son's son, husband/wife.

(*v*) He/She has no property (movable or immovable) and has no source of income.

Note 1—Any movable or immovable property which is not a source of income or profit shall *not* be regarded as a source of income. For example, the person concerned may be having a small house or hut but if this does not provide him or her with any profit by way of rent, etc. it shall not be counted as a source of income.

Note 2—The fact that an apparently supportless person has been able to survive and eke out a living due to relatives' charity either in cash or in kind, etc. shall not be a factor going against him or her for getting benefit under this scheme.

4. *Rate of financial assistance*—The rate of financial assistance shall uniformly be Rs. 60 per month per person. However, where there are more than two destitute or physically-handicapped persons in a family living together, the total financial assistance admissible to the family as a whole shall not exceed Rs. 150 per month.

5. *Kinds of financial assistance*—The financial assistance will be of two kinds, namely, (i) 'Financial Assistance for Life' (Life Assistance) and (ii) 'Financial Assistance for Limited Period' (Limited Period Assistance). Limited Period Assistance shall be for a specified period which shall terminate on attainment of the age of 18 years by any of the relatives or when such a relative as mentioned in rule 3(iv) starts supporting the destitute or when the disease or disability is cured or when the widow is re-married.

6. *Procedure for submitting application by the applicant*—(i) An application for financial assistance under these Rules shall be made in duplicate in the appended form to the Talathi, or Gram Sevak/Assistant Gram Sevak or the Tahsildar of the area in which the applicant is residing.

(*ii*) The application shall be accompanied by relevant documents and certificates in support of the eligibility conditions mentioned in Rule No. 3 above. Such certificates or documents shall be obtained in duplicate by the applicant from the competent authorities mentioned below:—

(a) Age Certificate	–	School leaving certificate, or attested extract of birth register of Municipality or Gram Panchayat. In the absence of the above, the age certificate from Government Medical Officer would be sufficient.
(b) Disability/Disease Certificate	–	Civil Surgeon, Gazetted Medical Officer or Medical Officer attached to the Municipality or Primary Health Centre or Unit.
(c) Income/Property Certificate	–	Talathi or Tahsildar or Gram Sevak/Assistant Gram Sevak.
(d) Destitution and having no relative as specified under Rule 3(iv)	–	Talathi or Gram Sevak/Assistant Gram Sevak or Gazetted Officer of State or Central Government.
(e) Certificate regarding non-begging or mendicancy	–	Talathi or Tahsildar or Assistant Gram Sevak or Gazetted Officer of State or Central Government.
(f) Certificate regarding not being an inmate of any Government or Charitable Institution or Home	–	Talathi or Tahsildar or Assistant Gram Sevak or Gazetted Officer of State or Central Government.
(g) Certificate of residency	–	Talathi or Tahsildar or Assistant Gram Sevak or District Magistrate.

7. *Sanctioning and disbursement of financial assistance*—(i) (a) Under these Rules financial assistance shall be sanctioned by a Committee in each Taluka consisting of 5 non-official members to be appointed by Government. Out of these 5 non-official members, one will be appointed as the Chairman of the Committeee by Government. Tahsildars of each Taluka will be secretary of this Committee.

(b) In respect of all Municipal areas and 'A' class Municipal areas there shall be a committee as mentioned in sub-rule (i)(a) above in each Legislative Assembly Constituency.

(ii) Disbursement of financial assistance to a beneficiary shall be made by the Tahsildar every month. However, in the case of Life Financial Assistance, the beneficiary shall intimate once in a year to the Tahsildar that he is alive and that there is no change in his case in any conditions of eligibility specified in Rule 3, residential address, etc. The same procedure will be followed in the case of Limited Period Assistance, but the intimation to the Tahsildar by the beneficiary on the above counts, namely, 'being alive' and 'no-change' in any eligibility conditions, etc. shall be made once in every six months. The financial assistance shall be discontinued forthwith if the beneficiary migrates to another State.

(*iii*) All payments of financial assistance shall be made to the applicants by Money Orders, such Money Orders being issued on the 26th of each month so that the beneficiary receives the Money Order before 3rd day of the following month. The cost on account of Money Order charges shall be borne by Government and will be met from the financial allotments placed at the disposal of the Tahsildars. It shall be the responsibility of the Director of Social Welfare to place the necessary allotment of funds at the disposal of the Collectors based on the requirements of the Tahsildars. The Collectors shall also be responsible for ensuring proper expenditure out of the allotment, maintenance of accounts, internal auditing of such accounts, etc. The Collector in this connection shall forward a quarterly report to the Director of Social Welfare and Government in Social Welfare Department.

(*iv*) *It shall be the responsibility of the tahsildar to process all applications for financial assistance received by him within a period of two weeks* at the maximum.

8. *Processing of Applications received by the Tahsildars* —All applications received by the concerned Tahsildar shall be arranged in an alphabetical order in a Register after giving Code No. etc. as per detailed procedure to be prescribed by the Director of Social Welfare.

9. *Right of appeal*—An appeal against the decision taken by the Committee at Taluka level/Legislative Assembly Constituency level mentioned in Rule 7(i) above shall lie with the State Level Committee to be appointed by Government in this behalf. This Committee at the State level shall consist of officials and non-officials and the decision taken by the State Level Committee shall be final.

10. *Intimation about death*—(*i*) If the beneficiary dies, the Village Officer in the case of Gram Panchayat area or the Municipal Authority in the case of Municipal area, shall report the fact to the Tahsildar immediately after the death occurs. The Tahsildars should make note of the fact of death in their register of financial assistance, resulting in stoppage of assistance forthwith.

(*ii*) In the case of death of the beneficiary the arrears of financial assistance computed till the date of the death shall be paid in deserving cases to the survivors if the beneficiary has a living wife or any of the relatives mentioned in Rule 3(iv) above 18 years of age and not having any employment or source of income.

11. *Miscellaneous*—(i) *Grant of Financial Assistance*—The grant of financial assistance under these Rules is a matter of absolute discretion of Government and may be refused or stopped, with or without giving any reasons by the sanctioning authority. The decision of the sanctioning authority shall not be liable to be questioned in any Court of Law and no suit or proceeding shall lie in any Court of Law.

(*ii*) Financial Assistance under these Rules shall not be liable to attachment under any process of Law.

(*iii*) The financial assistance sanctioned on mistaken grounds or on false information is liable to cancellation.

7

Case-Studies

In the final chapter a few case-studies are presented. These have been compiled by the team of four investigators and are based on answers to a questionnaire administered to those interviewed. The studies cover (*i*) the elderly who are institutionalized and (*ii*) those residing in the villages of Maharashtra. None of the cases deal with old persons from urban areas not living in institutions. This is a lacuna which our budget prevented us from filling.

In order to make sense of the large amount of material collected, it needs to be organized and categorized to a certain extent. At the same time, the immediacy of individual cases should be highlighted. The statistical data presented and analyzed in the earlier chapters, while illuminating the community of the old in general, do not give an idea about the living conditions and problems of individual elderly persons. The case-studies presented here aim to fill this gap.

In both the above-mentioned groups, three categories of the elderly were studied: the comparatively well off, the blind or handicapped, and the completely destitute for whom the institution is a haven of content. We shall begin with cases drawn from various OAHs, including the Home for Blind Women and the convalescent home at Dhairi attached to it. A very important factor in assessing the peace of mind of the elderly is the relationship with their families. However, perhaps the most significant and overriding factor is temperament, which shapes the ways in which the elderly

face their many physical, emotional and psychological problems.
[The author's comments are placed in square brackets].

1. A well-known actress of the thirties earned both reputation and
good money for a period of about 15 years. However, her husband
and son helped her squander it. By the time she was 57 it was all
gone, and she was abandoned by her family. After an unhappy 20
years of moving from place to place, she found solace in an old-age
home. The state gave her an artist's pension of Rs. 300 and some
philanthropists contributed the extra Rs. 150 required to make up
the amount to be paid for her upkeep. [Here is an example of a
person who had enjoyed a comfortable life. Unhappy experiences
forced her to enter an OAH, but in it she found peace and
contentment.]

2. An elderly couple, aged 77 and 73, are settled and working in
an OAH. The husband had retired from his job and owned a flat.
When their only son was killed in an accident, they decided to
spend the rest of their lives helping others. They sold their flat and
bought a two-room apartment on the premises of an OAH. Their
meals are provided by the OAH for which they pay Rs. 450 each.
Apart from handling various outside chores of the OAH, including
marketing, the husband helps distribute hot water to the inmates
for their baths. When necessary, he takes food and medicines to
the bedridden. The wife looks after the kitchen, makes suggestions
for improving the food, and sees that staff and inmates' needs
are taken care of. [In this way, the couple keep themselves busy
and care for the residents of the home as if they were their own
family. They have overcome their sorrow of losing their son in the
satisfaction of helping others.]

3. A Brahmin widower aged 88 lost his wife six years ago. He has
four sons and a daughter, but did not get on with any of them. He
used to be well-to-do with a big house, agricultural land, and a
moneylending business. He preferred to live with a friend in the
village rather than with his sons. This friend brought him to the
OAH when the old man was 85. He had no savings. Probably, his
sons cheated him in his old age and he lost a lot of money. He sued
his sons in court for maintenance and was proud of the fact. He is
the only man in the home where he stays. He does not get on with

the women there nor with anybody else, and spends his time reading, writing and going for walks on his own. [This old man has never learnt how to make friends. He is going to regret this as he gets older and more isolated.]

4. Rajanibai, 60 years old, is unmarried. She was educated up to the sixth standard. Then she realized that she could not see properly. When her parents came to know of her blindness, she was kept inside the home and not allowed to meet anybody. They felt that if it were known that she was going blind, they would not be able to get her married. However, being kept inside the four walls of the home led to a serious decline in her health. Her bones became brittle and her blindness incurable. Her two brothers and sisters-in-law were very kind to her, and cared for her after her parents died. She was put into the Women's Home for the Blind at the age of 30 along with others much older. She is happy in the Home and admires the institution. [One feels indignant at the thought of such callous treatment by society; especially the parents who condemned their daughter to a confined and unhappy life.]

5. Mrs. V is a 66-year-old, blind, married woman. As a young woman she used to teach music, but after her marriage to a politician and social worker she has led a very unhappy life. She was completely neglected by her husband; gave birth to five sons, all of whom died; and had to undergo many abortions. She became blind at the age of 50, and attributes it to her sorrows. No eye specialist was ever consulted. The husband thought it beneath his position to allow her to be institutionalized. However, some of his friends who were sympathetic to the wife suggested that she could do some social work in a Home for the Blind by teaching music to the women. In this way she was admitted to the home. She continues to feel very bitter about her husband, politicians and social workers. She has requested her husband to return her share of money so that she can donate it to the home but is very doubtful as to whether he will comply with her last request. [Such a marriage forces one to question the status of women in our society, and the hypocrisy of those who claim to be social workers.]

6. A blind widower, 78 years old, has been in an OAH for 6 years. He had served in the army as an electrical mechanic for 10 years. He then joined Ruston Company near Pune as a mechanical fitter for another 15 years. After retirement he became blind. He had not been aware of any problem and had not consulted a doctor. He had three sons, all of whom were living in one-room tenements. None of them wanted to keep him and he felt he was being insulted the whole time. His wife stayed with one of their sons and did not bother about him. After her death they did not even visit him in the OAH. He tries to get rid of his anger and feels that at least in the OAH he is not insulted. He says, 'Everything is okay. I have to live as long as ordained by God.' [This and other histories illustrate the ignorance and neglect of the blind by their own families, especially if they happen to be women. In some cases the families get the girl married without informing the husband's family that the girl is blind, leading to her ill-treatment at the hands of her in-laws. No medical advice is sought, and unscientific reasons are suggested for blindness.]

7. Mr. S is a married Muslim gentleman aged 60. He has three sons and two daughters, all quite young. He used to work in the Octroi Office. When he was 50, it was discovered that he had leprosy. He got himself treated at a leprosy hospital and was completely cured, but his family refused to take him back. He sought shelter in an OAH. After a while, when he was accepted by the inmates, he started working in the garden and keeping himself busy with outdoor work. In the home he has found the refuge denied to him by his own family.

8. Mrs. S is a 75-year-old Jain woman. She was widowed at the age of 52 and is childless. Her husband's savings were appropriated by some relatives so she became destitute. At first she used to work as a domestic help and was given food in return; she received no wages and had nowhere to live. For 22 years she slept in a temple at night; during this period she contracted diabetes and high blood pressure. After some treatment she developed cancer which was declared uncurable. Finally, she was admitted to an OAH where she is very well cared for. [If it were not for the attention of the staff and inmates of the OAH, this destitute woman would have died on the streets.]

9. An illiterate widow, 70 years of age, comes from a family of gardeners. She had five sons and one daughter; all the sons died before they were a year old; her daughter is mentally disturbed and was put into a mental home. This lady and her husband worked hard all their lives but rarely earned enough to eat properly. When the husband died six years ago, she tried to continue working but could not do so. Her employer brought her to the OAH where for the first time in her life she could eat her fill. She is content and only wishes for good health so that she remains mobile. She cannot think of leaving the home. [We now cite two cases of individuals who have shown unusual courage in rehabilitating themselves after disappointments and bereavements, and at the same time in contributing to the life of the community in OAHs.]

10. Mrs. R, 81 years old, was widowed at the age of 40. She has no children. Her husband was a doctor and she used to work with him as a compounder. After his death she studied medicine and ran the dispensary until she was 75 years old. She gets on well with her brother, sister and sister-in-law and would have been welcome in their homes. However, not wishing to burden them as they are also elderly, she chose to stay in an OAH.

She sold her large 12-room house and deposited the money in a bank account. With the interest she pays for her own upkeep in the home. At peace with herself, she is a very capable and good-natured person. She is helpful, gives advice when solicited, and is much admired, respected and welcome everywhere.

11. Mrs. V, 72 years old, was widowed 15 years ago. She was born in a village in a coastal district and had studied only up to the third standard. She has two children, a son and a daughter. After they were married, she decided to educate herself further and started studying. She appeared for the twelfth standard examination at the age of 60 and passed it; and then went on to graduate at the university. She wrote her autobiography. She now lives in the OAH at Hingane and looks after the garden. [This is an outstanding example of how a person can triumph over adverse circumstances and lead a happy and full life.]

We continue with examples of elderly persons living in villages: well-to-do, handicapped, destitute with or without pension; unusual examples of easy/difficult temperament, in that order.

12. An unmarred lady doctor, aged 73, was a gold medalist. Since she had no parents, she had looked after her two younger brothers and a sister. She had also saved for her old age. She used to get a monthly salary of Rs. 2,000. She did not marry because somebody had to take care of her brothers' and sister's education. She helped them and worked for them. But when they grew up they no longer needed her. When she retired at 58, they drove her out of the house. She tried to live on her own for seven years, but at the age of 65 she developed a blood pressure problem. She started becoming forgetful and lost confidence. So with her savings she joined an old-age home. But she is very diffident now. At the age of 73, she has totally forgotten her medical degree and medical skills. [Here is an example of a highly skilled educated person who totally neglected her personal life, namely marriage or love. Now she has nobody to love nor has she any moral support except the OAH. How could she not foresee this when young? At present she has the gold medal and savings but her life is empty and lonely.]

13. Mr. X 71 years old, is a well-to-do farmer. He owns 20 acres of land. Seven years ago his wife left him, but he does not seem to care. He had two sons and a daughter, but only one son is alive. He is 42 years old and lives elsewhere. The old man lives alone in his three-room house, brings fuel and water, and cooks for himself. He can no longer work on the farm but can use whatever grows without too much effort. He is educated enough to be able to read the newspapers. Though he has no friends, he is quite content with his life and has no worries.

14. Ms. K is an example of a person not usually found in a village. Sixty-two years old and highly educated, she worked as an educationist for 27 years. Since her retirement she has been receiving a pension of Rs. 1,361 a month. Thus, she has no financial problems. Her mother and her sister's son live with her in her four-room house. She suffers from arthritis and anaemia but does not worry too much about her health. Although she does not seem to be on the same wavelength as her neighbours, she has started an institution for helping the village women, and seems happy at being able to do something useful. She keeps herself busy and is contented with her life.

15. An elderly lady of 80 has been widowed for 35 years. She and her husband owned 80 acres of land and had one daughter. After her husband's death, the old lady sold the land and invested the money. When her daughter came of age, she got her married and helped her son-in-law to buy land. The young couple work on the land, and the old lady looks after their son. She cannot work any more and is cared for by her family. She would never think in terms of going to an OAH.

16. A 75-year-old carpenter is suffering from leprosy. He still works hard to earn enough to feed himself and his 68-year old wife. They have a two-room house. The couple have children—two sons and two daughters who live separately and do not help their parents. The old man is encouraged by his sympathetic wife. He is not sure how long he can continue to work. When asked how they will manage in future, he replies that they will depend on their village neighbours who will not let them starve.

17. This old man aged 65 has leprosy. When he first showed signs of the disease 20 years ago, his wife left him and married again. Of his three sons, only one has survived. He and his wife look after the old man as well as they can. He used to work as an agricultural labourer, but now having lost both hands and feet, he can only keep an eye on the family cattle. His son has three children. Working as agricultural labourers, he and his wife cheerfully support their own family as well as the handicapped father. All of them, including the children, are very kind and helpful to the old man who is completely disabled. [Here is another case of a heavy burden on the young who take on the responsibility of looking after the handicapped.]

18. The old couple are 84 and 80 years old respectively. He suffers from filaria and has occasional spells of fever and cannot work. His wife has become grumpy, and so the couple do not get on well together. They have a son and a daughter. The son is only 50 but is disabled and cannot do any work apart from looking after the cattle; his wife is dead. He has three children aged 18, 16 and 14. The 16-year-old daughter is married, and the 14-year-old girl attends school. Thus it is the 18-year-old grandson who has to shoulder the responsibility of managing the farm and supporting three disabled persons.

Earlier the family was quite well off. They had 12 acres of land, cattle, two houses, and a bullock cart. Some cattle had to be sold to get the granddaughter married. Four acres of land were displaced by a dam constructed on their land. One acre of land, one house, and the remaining cattle had to be sold whenever money was needed. The old man is full of worries and looks forward to his death. [In cases such as the above where families suffer due to very straitened financial circumstances, a pension or a similar scheme would be of great help.]

[We cite some instances where pensions are received, or where deserving persons are ineligible to get them.]

19. This old lady of 67 receives Rs. 100 a month from the Sanjay Niradhar Yojana. She has been widowed for a very long time and has no children. She used to work as a casual labourer and support herself; but with age she cannot go long distances for work. She collects cow-dung and makes dung-cakes which she sells, but often cannot earn enough to feed herself. Though her neighbours help her out, she questions, 'Why should I remain alive? Is it just to eat?' She is illiterate but thoughtful and aware.

20. An old childless widow, 66 years old, is suffering from leprosy. She cannot move and lies alone in her hut. She belongs to the shepherd class and used to rear sheep, but has never worked after the age of 50. She used to go around begging for her food and was not allowed to starve by her neighbours in the village. Now she gets Rs. 100 a month from the Sanjay Niradhar Yojana which she can use to buy food from her neighbours.

[We now cite two cases of needy persons who do not qualify for assistance.]

21. A widow from the backward class is 65 years old. Her only daughter is married, and her two sons earn well but live separately and do not help their mother who lives alone. She used to be able to do manual labour in the village and support herself; now she can only do light work for which she gets food and old clothes. When she is asked what she will do when disabled, she replies that she will go to the 'government'. Since she has two grown-up able-bodied sons she is ineligible for a pension but does not realise this.

22. A leper, aged 66 from a backward class, is very handicapped. He has lost both eyes and his nose. His wife is reportedly mentally disturbed. Out of their four children, two are alive, aged 15 and

17, and go to school. Though the wife can work a little, she finds it difficult to support four persons. The family has to be helped out by the villagers. Because the wife is capable of earning, the family is ineligible for a pension, according to the rules of the Sanjay Niradhar Yojana (see Appendix 6.1).

23. He is a widower, 70 years old, educated up to the seventh standard, relatively cultured and aware of the world around him. He cannot work hard but continues to do whatever he can. He has two sons and four daughters—will not give details of those who have died. His children and grandchildren are all educated and he has discouraged them from pursuing agriculture. Of the 30 acres of land and much livestock he had, he has sold 10 acres and nearly all the cattle. His grandson is an engineer and his granddaughter a university graduate.

He does not want to talk about his problems because he feels it would be useless. He is very critical of the government and political leaders, convinced that he will get no help from them. He feels that the government ought to provide employment for the young. [Here is an example of an experienced person from the rural areas who has definite views on what is required to help people to become independent. He would not consider going to an OAH under any circumstances].

24. The husband is 71 and the wife 66, and the couple have five sons and one daughter. She lives at home with her parents even though she is married; no reasons are given for this.

The old man used to work in Bombay in a textile mill until he was 62; now he cannot do hard work but looks after the cattle. He has 2 acres of land and two houses. He emphasized the importance of education, and all his sons are educated and well-placed. He lives with two sons and daughters-in-law, three grandchildren, and his wife and daughter. He is content. When asked whether he has saved for his old age, he replies that he has spent all his earnings on his children's education and now has no worries. He has full faith in them. [This couple with well-settled children is confident that the children will take care of them when old.]

25. This 80-year-old Kanarese man left his state and home 40 years ago when his wife died. He has no children. He took up employment as a *saaldaar*, (one who works on an annual basis of payment and receives food and cash from the employer). He used to allege that he is distantly related to his employer.

Now he is old and cannot work hard or see very well. He looks after the cattle. He gets his food twice a day, and when ill is given medicine. On the whole he has good health and does not complain about his arthritis. When asked what he would do when completely disabled, he replied that he was certain that he would be looked after by his employers. He is content and has no problems. [This person has been well-cared for by his employers.]

[As seen in the earlier chapters, the attitude to institutional care among the elderly differs very widely between those who reside in urban OAHs and those living in rural areas.]

References

Andrews, G.R., et al. 1986. *Aging in the Western Pacific: A Four Country Study*. Manila: WHO Regional Office for Western Pacific.

Bose, Ashish. 1982. 'Aspects of Aging in India.' Paper presented at the Asian Regional Conference on Active Aging: The Elderly of Asia organized by the Social Research Centre. Manila.

Brody, Elaine M., Pauline T. Johnsen, Mark C. Fulcomer, and **Abigail M. Lang.** 'Women's Changing Roles and Help to Elderly Parents.' In B.C. Miller and D.H. Olson, eds., *Family Studies Review Yearbook*, vol. 3. Beverly Hills: Sage Publications.

Chanana, H.B. and **P.P. Talwar.** 1987. 'Aging in India: Its Socio-economic and Health Implications.' *Asia-Pacific Population Journal*. 3 (2): 23–38.

Choe, Ehn Hyum. 1992. 'New Role of Elderly in Newly Industrializing Countries.' Paper presented at the Conference on Local Level Policy Development to Deal with the Consequences of Population Aging organized by the International Federation on Aging and UN ESCAP. Pune: 1–4 September.

Dave, Chandra. 1992. 'Summary of the Government Programmes for the Aged in Various States.' Paper presented at the Global Conference on Aging organized by the International Federation on Aging and UN ESCAP. Pune.

Goel, S.L. and **R.K. Jain.** 1988. *Social Welfare Administration in India*, vols. 1 and 2. New Delhi: Deep and Deep Publications.

Government of India. 1988. *Family Welfare Programme in India Yearbook 1986–87*. New Delhi: Ministry of Health and Family Welfare, Government of India.

Hill, Reuben. 1965. 'Decision-Making and the Family Life Cycle.' In Ethel Shanas and Gordon Streib, eds., *Generational Relations*. Englewood Cliffs: Prentice Hall.

Indian Statistical Institute, Demographic Research Unit. 1986. *Reconstruction of Indian Life Tables for 1901–81 and Projections for 1981–2000*. Calcutta: Indian Statistical Institute.

International Labour Organization. 1979. *World Summary in ILO 65th Session: Older Workers' Work and Retirement*, vol. 5. Geneva: ILO.

Joshi, Mahadeo Shastri, eds., 1974. *Bharatiya Sanskriti Kosh*, vol. 8. New Delhi: Ministry of Education, Government of India and Pune: Government of Maharashtra.

Kono, Shigemi. 1977. 'The Concept of the Family Life Cycle As a Bridge between Demography and Sociology.' In IUSSP (International Union for Scientific Study of Population), Conference Mexico City, vol. 1., 2.2, 355–70.

Malaker and **Guha Roy**. 1986. *Population Estimates*. Calcutta: Indian Statistical Institute.

Miller, B.C. and **D.H. Olson**, eds., 1985. *Family Studies Review Yearbook* vol. 3. Beverly Hills: Sage Publications.

Nyedegger, Corinne N. 'Family Ties of the Aged in a Cross-Cultural Perspective.' In B.C. Miller and D.H. Olson, eds., *Family Studies Review Yearbook*, vol. 3. Beverly Hills: Sage Publications.

Pati, R.N. and **B. Jena**. 1989. *Aged in India*. New Delhi: Ashish Publishing.

Registrar-General. 1983. *Census of India 1981: Reports and Tables, Series I, India, Part II, Special*. Delhi: Controller of Publications.

Registrar-General. 1990. *Sample Registration System 1989*. New Delhi: Vital Statistics Division, Ministry of Home Affairs, Government of India.

Ryder, Norman B. 1965. 'The Cohort As a Concept in the Study of Social Change.' *American Sociological Review*. 30: 843–61.

Shanas, Ethel and **Gordon Streib**, eds. 1965. Generational Relations. Englewood Cliffs: Prentice Hall.

Stehonwer, Jan. 1965. 'Relations between Generations and the Three Generations in Denmark.' In Ethel Shanas and Gordon Streib, eds., *Generational Relations*. Englewood Cliffs: Prentice Hall.

Townsend, Peter. 1962. '*The Last Refuge*.' In David L. Sills, ed., *International Encyclopedia of the Social Sciences*, vol. 1–2. New York: Macmillan and Free Press, and London: Collier Macmillan.

United Nations. 1985. *World Population Prospects: Estimates and Projections as Assessed in 1982*. Population Studies No. 86. New York: United Nations.

United Nations. 1988. *World Demographic Estimates and Projections, 1950–2025*. New York: United Nations.

Ward, R.A. 1979. *The Aging Experience*. New York: J.B. Lippincott Co.